D1457332

Dream of a Word

THE TIA CHUCHA PRESS
POETRY ANTHOLOGY

Edited by
Quraysh Ali Lansana
and Toni Asante Lightfoot

Foreword by
Luis J. Rodríguez

TIA CHUCHA PRESS
LOS ANGELES

Copyright © 2005 by Tia Chucha Press. All rights revert to authors.

Printed in the United States of America

ISBN 1-882688-30-9

Book Design: Jane Brunette
Cover Painting: "Winter Spider" by Tony Fitzpatrick. Copyright © 2005 by Tony Fitzpatrick.
Tony Fitzpatrick appears courtesy of Pierogi Gallery.

Published by:

Tia Chucha Press
A Project of Tia Chucha's Centro Cultural
PO Box 328
San Fernando, CA 91341
www.tiachucha.com

Distributed by:

Northwestern University Press
Chicago Distribution Center
11030 South Langley Avenue
Chicago, IL 60628

Tia Chucha Press is supported by the National Endowment for the Arts and operating funds
from Tia Chucha's Centro Cultural. Tia Chucha's Café & Centro Cultural have received support
from the Los Angeles Department of Cultural Affairs, the Center for Cultural Innovation, the
Middleton Foundation, Not Just Us Foundation, the Liberty Hill Foundation, Youth Can
Service, Toyota Sales, Solidago Foundation, and other grants and donors including Bruce
Springsteen, John Densmore, Dan Attias, Dave Marsh, Suzan Erem, Cynthia Cuza, Denise
Chávez and John Randall of the Border Book Festival, and Luis & Trini Rodríguez.

To Melvin Dixon, Ricardo Sánchez, and John Sheehan:
Tia Chucha Press authors
who have joined the great ancestors

And Sue Ying
A founder and board member of the Guild Complex

as well as all the artists, poets, and other victims
of Hurricane Katrina, August-September, 2005

CONTENTS

9   Foreword / *Luis J. Rodríguez*

13   Introduction / *Quraysh Ali Lansana and Toni Asante Lightfoot*

I. THE STARS AND STRIPES STRIPPED

21   Pledge of America / *Diane Glancy*

22   In A Tar-Mangled Manner / *Rohan B Preston*

23   Workers / *David Hernández*

25   First Day / *Angela Shannon*

26   JFK for a Day: The Tour / *Virgil Suárez*

28   Marquette Park, 1966 / *Gale Renee Walden*

31   Song for the Nineties / *John Sheehan*

32   Exquisite Politics / *Denise Duhamel & Maureen Seaton*

33   Rave Politics / *ariel robello*

34   Everyone's Living Room / *Gale Renee Walden*

35   Brain on Ice: The El Train Poem / *Michael Warr*

37   A School Yard of Broken Dreams / *Marvin Tate*

38   explode / *Mary Kathleen Hawley*

39   It's Not the Heat, It's the Stupidity / *Carlos Cumpián*

41   Tomatoes / *Luis J. Rodríguez*

43   Armadillo Charm / *Carlos Cumpián*

46   El Grupo McDonald's / *Nick Carbó*

47   Velvet / *Cin Salach*

II. AN ACHING MOSIAC

50   We Are a People Quite Integral / *Ricardo Sánchez*

51   Freeing the Fossil / *Cin Salach*

53   Scattering Dreams / *Angela Shannon*

54   In An American Landscape / *Kyoko Mori*

56   Exquisite Minority / *Denise Duhamel & Maureen Seaton*

57   Good to Her / *Jean Howard*

59   jeunes filles / *Zada Johnson*

60   What I'm Telling You / *Elizabeth Alexander*

61   Of Fish / *Mary Kathleen Hawley*

62   Mt. Zion Baptist / *Afaa M. Weaver*

63   Why Couldn't I Have Been Born A Baptist? / *Michael Warr*

64   I Am the Fourth Supreme / *Lisa Buscani*

65   Public Radio Plays Eddie Harris / *A. Van Jordan*

66   Derrick Poem (The Lost World) / *Terrance Hayes*

67   Notes for a Poem on Being Asian American / *Dwight Okita*

69   Welcome / *David Hernández*

III. MADE FROM GHOSTS

73   Two Daughters / *Josie Raney*

74   Miscarry / *Anne-Marie Cusac*

75   Poem for The Unnamed / *Dwight Okita*

76   I take all my troubles / *Sterling D. Plumpp*

78   Blues for My Daddy / *Zada Johnson*

80   Fathers / *Michael R. Brown*

81   On the Fourth of July.... / *Tony Fitzpatrick*

83   The Killing Floor / *Andres Rodríguez*

84   Gutters / *Josie Raney*

85   Disorganization / *Michael R. Brown*

87   Turning Forty in the 90's / *Melvin Dixon*

88   Trace / *Virgil Suárez*

89   The Dead Still Walk... / *Tony Fitzpatrick*

91   Letter from Foreign / *Rohan B Preston*

92   The Monster / *Luis J. Rodríguez*

93   Battle / *ariel robello*

94   Homecoming / *Andres Rodríguez*

96   Hearing about the Mystery Lights on a Bus
     near Joplin / *Diane Glancy*

97   Pretending the Ghost / *Patricia Smith*

99   Cough Medicine / *Elizabeth Alexander*

100   Thoughts of an Ambivalent Carnivore / *John Sheehan*

IV. BENEATH THE CLATTER

103   Night Train / *Anne Marie Cusac*

104   Insomnia in N.Y.C. / *Marvin Tate*

106   Daybreak Wakes / *Sterling D. Plumpp*

108   Eating In Anger / *Kyoko Mori*

110   When The Neighbors Fight / *Terrance Hayes*

111   Halloween / *Mike Puican*

112   Boy Sneezes, Head Explodes / *Patricia Smith*

114   To Be Heard / *Lisa Buscani*

116   Ang Tunay Na Lalaki Receives
      Instructions for His Last Workshop Poem / *Nick Carbó*

118   Automatic Writing / *Mike Piucan*

119   "Convicts, Inmates & Felons, Too..." / *Ricardo Sánchez*

121   The Lifestory Of Eddie James "Son" House Jr.
      As Told Through His Hands / *A. Van Jordan*

122   Little Girls, 1993 / *Afaa M. Weaver*

123   Dancing in Your Mother's Skin / *Jean Howard*

125   Spring Cleaning / *Melvin Dixon*

126   Appendix: Study Questions

144   List of Tia Chucha Press Books

146   About the Contributors

150   About the Editors

FOREWORD

ITLATOL TEMICTLI – the dream of a word. It's an ancient Mexika (Aztec) concept – here it is, in text translated from a pre-Columbian codex: *And, O friends, hear the dream of a word: Each spring gives us life, the golden ear of corn refreshes us, the tender ear of corn becomes a necklace for us. We know that the hearts of our friends are true!*

Everything, every idea, every energy has its duality. A spirit to the thing. A person has a dream, so does a tree. A dual life. One is part of the "other world," the place of ancestors, eternal time, memory. The other is part of the temporal, waking, touch world. Both are real to the Mexikas.

Every word therefore has its dream.

Once I attended a literary gathering and a poet at my table made the inane comment: "The Aztecs were destroyed because they had no poetry."

The fact that she was of European descent, and privileged in the way race and class dominance works in the US, added to the insult. The Mexikas were integrally poetic. They were artistic, scientific, and spiritually bound. For them, all three aspects were connected – the same. The more they studied nature and the sky – and built their fantastic structures to the rhythms of the stars and earth's fertile cycles – the more they found the sacred. When they created statues, songs, poems, dances, temples, bridges, causeways, gardens, and plumed head dresses, they experienced the sacred. There was no separation between the internal and the external, science and the spiritual, being awake and the dream.

Dream of the Word: The Tia Chucha Press Poetry Anthology consists of poetry from the 40 or so volumes of books and chapbooks we've done since 1989; we want to carry on with this concept, this tradition, this centuries-old conversation to recognize the word and its dream.

I began Tia Chucha Press in the fall of 1989 when I received funds from the Chicago Department of Cultural Affairs to do my first book, *Poems across the Pavement*. The Puerto Rican artist, Gamaliel Ramirez, gave me a beautiful drawing for the cover. Jane Brunette, a Menominee-European writer and graphic designer, designed the book (at the time, we both worked for the Archdiocese of Chicago's Liturgy Training Publications; Jane has been Tia Chucha Press' main book designer ever since).

Soon Chicago-area poets requested I publish their manuscripts. By then, I was active in the Chicago poetry scene – home of the internationally renowned Poetry Slams and other poetry-based creations. Over the years, Tia Chucha Press published local luminaries like Patricia Smith, David Hernández, Michael Warr, Rohan B Preston, Carlos Cumpían, Jean Howard, Dwight Okita, Cin Salach, Lisa Buscani, and Tony Fitzpatrick. In 1991, we merged with the Guild Complex, a leading arts and literary presentation organization I helped found, and led by Michael Warr, my friend and fellow poet. With Northwestern University Press eventually becoming our distributor, our books appeared on bookshelves in bookstores, libraries, and book festivals around the country. We soon received manuscripts from all corners of the land. We ended up publishing the poetry collections of well-known writers such as Elizabeth Alexander, Afaa Weaver, Kyoko Mori, Diane Glancy, Melvin Dixon, Nick Carbó, and Ricardo Sánchez. We also broke out the first books of amazing poets such as A. Van Jordan, Terrance Hayes, Andres Rodríguez, Anne-Marie Cusac, Angela Shannon, and ariel robello.

In addition, we published a number of anthologies such as *Power Lines, Stray Bullets, Open Fist, Shards of Light/Astillas de luz* as well as youth work from Chicago's Gallery 37's literary workshops. In 1994, we created a CD of poetry and music collaborations with Chicago poets called *A Snake in the Heart*. And in 2004, we did chapbooks of Chicago poets Josie Raney, Michael Puican and Zada Johnson.

Our writers have won major recognition in the poetry world – including National Poetry Slams, a Lila Wallace-Reader's Digest Writers Award, Whiting Writers Fellowships, a King-Tufts Discovery Award, PEN USA Josephine Miles Literary Awards, a Poetry Center Book Award, and National Endowment for the Arts fellowships, among others.

In 2005, Tia Chucha Press moved its operations to Los Angeles, California to join the not-for-profit Tia Chucha's Centro Cultural that I helped start in the San Fernando Valley section of the city. This is the sister organization to the bookstore, café, art gallery, performance space, and cyber café called Tia Chucha's Café Cultural (founded by my wife Trini, my brother-in-law Enrique Sánchez, and myself about a year-a-half after my family moved to LA in the summer of 2000).

How better to honor these fantastic voices – of diverse backgrounds and styles, nationalities and cultures – than to have an anthology of their work with the aim of having them read and discussed in classrooms throughout the country.

Quraysh Ali Lansana is the ideal editor – a poet and professor, who has been a champion of Tia Chucha Press and on our editorial board for at least a decade. With the crucial assistance of Toni Asante Lightfoot, the book realized its dream, its final direction and shape.

Tia Chucha Press came out of a movement and a cause – to democratize poetry and help make poetry central to US culture (instead of war, social division, material gain, polarized politics, and a media catering to the lowest common denominator in the culture). We need poetry more than ever. As long as poetry continues to be pushed to the fringes of our culture, and perhaps forgotten, we remain in deep spiritual peril.

It's been sixteen years since we first started. Without our authors' hard work, the Guild Complex, our tireless editorial board (that has consisted, at one time or another, of Reginald Gibbons, Michael Warr, Julie Parson-Nesbitt, Mary Kathleen Hawley, Mark Ingebretsen, Olga Herrera, Rohan B. Preston, and Quraysh Ali Lansana), Tia Chucha's Café & Centro Cultural, my family, and the lovers of poetry everywhere, we wouldn't be here. Here's a gift, then, to keep poetry alive; to make poetry an every-day, every-occasion thing; and to the dream that is our word.

The word that is our dream.

■ LUIS J. RODRÍGUEZ
FOUNDER/EDITOR,
TIA CHUCHA PRESS

INTRODUCTION

Once the poet was our spokesman, and not our oracle, our advocate and not our secret
agent, or at least he or she was as much the one as the other; and if the poet did not speak
for us, all of us, fully and warmly, if the poems lacked the larger vision of humanity, we said
he or she was deficient in one of the qualities which, virtually by definition, make a poet.

HAYDEN CARRUTH,

FROM *POETS WITHOUT PROPHECY*

*H*AS POETRY become fast food?

If we were to measure the current state of contemporary American
poetics against Mr. Carruth's statement, we would find most poets woefully
negligent on the "vision of humanity" issue, and most presses whoring with
pop culture.

From within its blistering veins, the irregular pulse of the US of
America, sick with superficiality and immediacy, drunk on quick political
fixes, is also the incubator of vibrancy, ingenuity, and survival. This experi-
ment would receive a C-minus at the Science Fair for Humankind. Passing,
but only by a chad.

Nevertheless, it is this lack of linear syncopation, this Thelonius
Monk of a heart-thump, which enables most of us to breathe, to stay alive, to
not commit to a life of crime. This is why, as noted poet and publisher Haki
Madhubuti put it, "poets are not legislators." We exist in the kennings, the
tiny space between. Thus, the depth of meaning when Chicago writer and Tia
Chucha Press author David Hernández refers to himself as a "famous poet."
Does movement outside of this void kill the artist? It doesn't have to, but
again, check who's sleeping with the canon.

Doesn't the canon exist to be blasted, to be fired, shot up? Expanded?

Sure, you're thinking, "Now the editors of this anthology are going to distance themselves from the throngs of milquetoast verse and call into question everything published in the last fifty years."

This is unnecessary. Luis J. Rodríguez and the thirty-six (and counting) Tia Chucha Press authors have already done so:

> ...Politics is a grain of rice stuck in the mouth
> of a king. I voted for a clump of cells,
> anything to believe in, true as rain, sure as red wheat.
> I carried my ballots around like smokes, pondered big questions,
> resources and need, stars and planets, prehistoric
> languages....
>
> FROM *EXQUISITE POLITICS* BY DENISE DUHAMEL
> AND MAUREEN SEATON

Tia Chucha Press has provided a pulpit for diverse ideas and aesthetics since 1989, providing a committed vehicle for poets to publish their truths in their ways. These voices, both tender and gritty, slam poets and academics, originate with gentle urgency from the barrio:

> Papi worked the factory
> for 25 years he worked
> leaving his drop of sweat
> deeper than the ocean.
> He would replenish his dream
> wipe off the sense of not belonging
> and think of mami
> on the other side of town
> working in the hospital...
>
> FROM *WORKERS* BY DAVID HERNÁNDEZ

with haunting desperation from Smallville, USA:

> This is what happens at night in Normal:
> children marry wrong, everyone quits smoking,
> and fathers love their daughters so fiercely
> everywhere it is quiet...
>
> FROM *EVERYONE'S LIVING ROOM* BY GALE RENEE WALDEN

and the concrete and steel urban adventure:

> They thought that the ball
> would never stop bouncing,
> stomping and jumping on the hot
> grey gravel, like giant gladiators
> ready for war
>
> in beat up All Stars and stolen Nikes
> gliding magically in the air, as if
> a modern ballet set to urban funk
>
> FROM *A SCHOOL YARD OF BROKEN DREAMS* BY MARVIN TATE

Tia Chucha Press possesses one of the most ethnically diverse booklists in contemporary letters. These books offer frank and fruitful explorations of race, class and gender issues, but never at the expense of adventurous, well-crafted verse. A quarter of TCP poets are first generation American writers, and the entire booklist is global in scope, reflecting authors who are American Indian & Filipino, Mexican & Jamaican, living in Massachusetts, California, and most points in between:

> Mum, you tell me that they have scholarships galore.
> And, a true. But you never say anything 'bout glass,
> 'bout aquarium and how buckra can encase you
> in glass so that no matter how loud you scream
> no matter how much you bark, the ceiling still there.
>
> FROM *LETTER FROM FOREIGN* BY ROHAN B PRESTON

Dream of a Word is a living archive, of not only one of the most significant poetry presses of the last century, but of the possibilities of the human condition.

This anthology contains poems by every poet who has published a single volume of poetry with Tia Chucha. We were unable to include poems by the many fine poets published in the six other TCP anthologies, but would like to acknowledge those great books and their editors:

Power Lines: A Decade of Poetry from Chicago's Guild Complex, edited by Julie Parson-Nesbitt, Luis J. Rodríguez and Michael Warr, 1999

shards of light/astillas de luz, edited by Olivia Maciel, 1998 *dream in yourself: a collection of literary works from gallery 37*, edited by Quraysh Ali Lansana and J.M. Morea, 1997

I Represent: A Collection of Literary Works from Gallery 37, edited by Quraysh Ali Lansana, 1996

Open Fist: An Anthology of Young Illinois Poets, edited by Anne Schultz, 1993

Stray Bullets: A Celebration of Chicago Saloon Poetry, edited by Ida Therese Jablanovec, Susen James and Jose Chávez, 1991

Dream of a Word is divided into five sections, grouped by theme. Section One—The Stars and Stripes Stripped contains poems that function on various levels as commentaries on the tumultuous political and social playing fields of contemporary society; Section Two—An Aching Mosaic consists of verse exploring ethnicity, culture, and how these two ethnographic elements manifest on an intimate, daily basis; Section Three—Made from Ghosts reveals poems that address family and relationships, and poems in Section Four— Beneath the Clatter discuss art, writing, dreams, and dissonance.

Section Five of the book includes a wealth of critical thinking strategies and writing prompts for every poem in the anthology. This book will enable the next generation of inspired poets by providing thought-provoking poems and study questions to further an understanding of prosody and ideas. This anthology is a teaching tool, a stepping stone for the imagination. These constructs have been at the core of Tia Chucha Press since its inception.

As we were wrapping up this anthology, the Gulf Coast of this country was ravaged by the most devastating natural disaster in U.S. history. Hurricane Katrina not only caused severe damage to homes and countless lives, it exposed the extent to which the Bush Administration was ill-prepared to handle emergency situations. How is it that the man appointed to head this nation's federal response for emergencies resigned after being sent packing, just hours before we learned his background was in the caretaking of show horses? This was more than a breach in the levee. It was a breach in the contract with the US government, a fissure in the project known as democracy. We dedicate this anthology to the numerous poets, artists, activists and others who lost their lives in the wake of this tragedy.

Dream of a Word is also dedicated to the deceased members of the

Tia Chucha Press and Guild Complex family, including poets Melvin Dixon, Ricardo Sánchez and John Sheehan, and long-time activist and visual artist Sue Ying, who was present at the old Guild Bookstore from the beginning. You are here. All of you.

Special thanks to our Assistant Editor, Randall Horton, for the long hours, elbow grease and commitment to detail. Additional thanks are due to our invaluable editorial assistants Derrick Harriell, Chanell Harris, and Timothy Seintz.

The Sheehan poem "Song for the Nineties," published in 1997, concludes:

> *Beware of the devil who lies inside*
> *your brother, your sister, yourself.*
>
> *Beware of talking with any of these,*
> *but beware the more if there is no talk.*

It is the poet's job to ask questions.
It is the poet's job to beware and be aware.

■ QURAYSH ALI LANSANA AND
TONI ASANTE LIGHTFOOT
SEPTEMBER 2005, CHICAGO

THE STARS

AND

STRIPES

STRIPPED

PLEDGE OF AMERICA

You got our squaw corn.
Stripped flint corn.
Red flour corn. Soft white corn.
Our blue corn.
Nuetta sweet corn. Pod corn.
Short ear dent corn.
The purple sunflower and pumpkin.
They're growing all over your yards and house.
The white lima bean.
Yellow bean. Pinto.
Calico bean.
Brown tepary bean.
Hominy and tobacco.
Yes. You got it all now in your furrows. You even know when light
says it will be another hour. You're the Hourists who thought of
time. You got it, Chickie. The whole wax. The Pow Wowists can't
sit back like you. *Whee Choo.* All tickies twanging for you. The
Great Hour of Hope is yours, baby. The Hipped. We're the humble
bee, Bubba. The Whipped. The stars and stripes stripped. The old
Geronimo death cry. No licorice stick for our sweet teeth. It's a
black rope lasso for us, cowpoke. Under your ingemious grip. You
even shut off dark. Bring lightbulbs to the night. Eyeballs of the
spirits. *Zote. Whazzotta!* Yours be do. Our burden basket.
Corniefields. Kachina carnie clowns. Indivisible. American Bull
says *Liberty be yous.*

■ DIANE GLANCY FROM *THE RELIEF OF AMERICA*

In a Tar-Mangled Manner

O, slave, can you flee
by the eagle's first flight
for so loudly we wail
from that whipper's fresh creaming,

who's brought swipes and blue scars
to our tremulous thighs
and our children, we watched,
O, so helplessly screaming?

O, the lynchers' red stare—
their licks bursting in fear
burned blood through the night,
the charred fruit is still there.

O, say, is that tar-mangled
planter, that slave,
still in the hands of debris
that have come from the caves?

■ ROHAN B PRESTON FROM *DREAMS IN SOY SAUCE*

WORKERS

Papi worked the factory
for 25 years he worked
leaving his drop of sweat
deeper than the ocean.
He would replenish his dream
wipe off the sense of not belonging
and think of mami
on the other side of town
working in the hospital
cleaning bedpans with full-strength
 ammonia and Ajax for institutional use only
   and made the beds with fresh sheets
    while the old/sick people saw her
       as an angel of mercy who understood their pain
        and she would smile a soothing smile
          that word got around that she was a real soft touch
           because she shed real tears when anyone
            left the hospital dead or alive
             and they loved her mucho because
              she would talk about her oldest son
               who woke up at 5 in the morning
                before going to Waller High School
                 and sweep and mop floors for a company
                  around Fullerton and Sheffield
                   and how he would give her 10 dollars-
                    a-week to help out with the groceries
                     and keep enough for the movies on Saturday
                      him and Manuel Perez who also worked hard
                       but they were bold and dared to ask
                       /is this the way forever?
                      Something better got to give/
                       as they watched all the upheaval and drama
                       on the screen but the movie was way deep
                        inside their hearts specially the ending
                        where all the badness got blown apart
                       and they left the theater

real happy and full of hope
that cold day of 1959
was never the same again
was never the same again.

■ DAVID HERNÁNDEZ FROM *ROOFTOP PIPER*

FIRST DAY

My sister and I crossed the train tracks
after school and started back on the dirt road,

gazing at the field of sunflowers, their stems
tall as giraffes reaching toward the possible.

Butterflies hopscotched on waving grass
while we skipped toward Miss Luella's biscuits.

And with every step, we disremembered
the National Guard pointing and ordering

the principal to open the school doors,
the girl with sausage curls spitting and crying,

the teacher re-naming us pickaninnies.
We rose when the bell trembled,

straightened our faces and spines, wrapped
our arms around each other's spirits

and forgave God for being absent-
minded and not meeting us that day.

■ ANGELA SHANNON FROM *SINGING THE BONES TOGETHER*

JFK FOR A DAY: THE TOUR

after the newspaper story

For $25 bucks, you can sit in the back
    of an open-top limousine, a 1964

Lincoln restored to look like the 1963
    model, make your way through Dealey

Plaza, hear the crack of rifle fire
    as you drive past the Texas School Book

Depository, feel the car speed up
    as it roars past the Grassy Knoll.

"From there, from there." says the guide,
    and points to where Zapruder stood,

camera in hand, then past the underpass
    toward Parkland Memorial Hospital.

The car, the tour, recreates the moment
    with piped-in sound effects and radio

broadcasts from the day the president
    was shot—the tour guide says no one

on the three trips a day on workdays,
    eight a day during the weekend, has found

the tour offensive. Many Dallas residents
    and city leaders have resisted annual

memorials to the assassination, a way
    to erase the shame. Next year, the guide

says he will have video monitors installed
    to show the moment when that crazy

bullet hit the back of Kennedy's head,
    and Jackie crawled over the trunk

to retrieve the flap of scalp before it blew away,
    a little extra, for the sake of verisimilitude.

■ VIRGIL SUÁREZ FROM *YOU COME SINGING*

MARQUETTE PARK, 1966

When the call came
my mother was washing her dyed hair
      in beer, as a conditioner & topic for gossip,
      alms for a congregation
who expected a preacher's wife
      to be thin with prayer & smell of
      orchids & gardenias.
But this was Saturday, it was lazy
      the Beatles were singing
how much they loved me.
      Outside in the streets the
neighborhood Polish
shouted frantic & loose
as children played hopscotch
      jumping down the block
to Sky Blue
where city trinkets were on display
and the butcher wrapped kielbasa
in white paper for barbecues.

The message on the phone was simple:
      they are coming to your church with the King
      they will want to go in and pray
      and suddenly my father was back
rushing around like the emergency of something about to happen
bolting next door to the church to unlock the double wooden doors
leading to Sanctuary.
My father was thirty-two and handsome
      and the clerical collar he wore
propped him up higher than the rest of us
      so that when he lifted me
I went all the way to the ceiling
      which was pretty close to God.
He didn't lift me that day; I was eight
      and getting harder to hold.
Three girls trailed him to the door
      trying to catch his legs
as he forgot to wave good-by.

When the first rock went through
the parsonage window
my mother reached for the phone
called June, the only neighbor she trusted
and my mother who never left the house without makeup or high-heels
who told me I'd be thirty before I'd understand the true beauty of lipstick
wrapped a towel around her head, barefoot opened the door
unto a crowd of people:
                    Butcher, Baker, Locksmith, Thief.
The woman two doors down
who wore pink cashmere
whose daughter was named
after a Christmas Carol was there.
She was the mother we all coveted
and I started to smile at her
but she had changed
into something way past herself
                    Nigger Lovers
she screamed.
My mother looked straight through her & expanded,
grew large enough to shelter us all below her skirts;
                    zig-zagged us
into the clear open Oz
                    of the city street
as we jumped the rough blacktop
into the thin hands of June.

June walked us up the third floor flat
and led us to the screened-in porch
where her daughter Karen waited.
The first shot was distant as a cork-pop.
We looked to Karen for guidance;
she was Catholic and we needed ritual
so we turned three times and faced East
and then we could see the shadowed,
distant surge of the crowd as they started
to rock Impalas as if they were toy models
in a Japanese horror film.

The shouting & cursing merged with the singing marchers
and the voices & songs echoed into us, becoming our own.
The marchers never got to the church
that day—the roads were blocked and
the city had started to burn again.
                    On Sunday the pews were empty in church and
                    my father preached the sermon
about loving your neighbor to his family alone
while my mother sang the hymns in
a thin, melodic line.
Outside the Christian Soldiers
                    marched onward
                    and the streets
rang out a music
            of guns
that never ended.

The children chose alternative codas:
                    some turning
themselves in early
                    taking their colors
to the graves.
Others didn't grow up
                    because they had seen the outcome
but none of us ever really went home again
to the city of our dreams
where the double-dutching
of black & white
                    was too pretty to leave
                    and the earnest prayers of children
Assured that it was not only the cinematic monster
Looming visible over skyscrapers
& small quilted farmlands
that was guaranteed, by the end, to fall.

■ GALE RENEE WALDEN FROM *SAME BLUE CHEVY*

SONG FOR THE NINETIES

Beware of the Arab, beware of the Jew,
beware of the English, the Irish,
the Tutsi, the Hutu,
the Serbs, the Croatians,
beware of the born-again Christian.

Beware of the Black, beware of the White,
beware of the students, the teachers,
the old, the young,
the rich, the poor,
beware the wild Indian swinging his tomahawk.

Beware the Catholic, beware the Protestant,
the atheist, the agnostic.
Beware the criminal, beware the police.
Beware of your friendly protectors,
the status quo, the avante garde,
beware the revolution.

Beware of the devil who lies inside
your brother, your sister, yourself.

Beware of talking with any of these,
but beware the more if there is no talk.

Just beware, Baby, beware.

■ JOHN SHEEHAN FROM *LEAVING GARY*

EXQUISITE POLITICS

The perfect voter has a smile but no eyes,
maybe not even a nose or hair on his or her toes,
maybe not even a single sperm cell, ovum, little paramecium.
Politics is a slug copulating in a Poughkeepsie garden.
Politics is a grain of rice stuck in the mouth
of a king. I voted for a clump of cells,
anything to believe in, true as rain, sure as red wheat.
I carried my ballots around like smokes, pondered big questions,
resources and need, stars and planets, prehistoric
languages. I sat on Alice's mushroom in Central Park,
smoked longingly in the direction of the mayor's mansion.
Someday I won't politic anymore, my big heart will stop
loving America and I'll leave her as easy as a marriage,
splitting our assets, hoping to get the advantage
before the other side yells: *Wow!* America,
Vespucci's first name and home of the free and brave, *Te amo.*

■ DENISE DUHAMEL AND MAUREEN SEATON
FROM *EXQUISITE POLITICS*

Rave Politics

you can look but don't touch the butterflies
an angel is a death trap with wings
space aliens are open to solicitations
white pills will make your skin peel off
the blue ones will put it back on
don't take a first date
if your friends multiply before your eyes
take off the glasses
if they grow another head
gently push it back in
a bad dancer is probably a Narc
not everybabydoe is looking at you
two is boring
three or more is showbiz
when you take off in the red balloon don't look down
when you land   don't look up
fire-breathing dragons will deflate
when driving into nowhere gas up and buy tic tacs
to   t r a i l   behind you
if glass shards spin all around
pretend they're sugar plum fairies
but whatever you do never
no never stop dancing

■ ARIEL ROBELLO FROM *MY SWEET UNCONDITIONAL*

EVERYONE'S LIVING ROOM

This is what happens at night in Normal:
children marry wrong, everyone quits smoking,
and fathers love their daughters so fiercely
everywhere it is quiet. In houses wrapped
with porches, rocking chairs are wearing treads
in wood as people remember the first time,
which has become your first time,
which has become your fear. Inside
telephones are ringing and people watch
the ten-o'clock news—there it is safe
to love sentimentally, there it is common
to fight without valor, and when a globe
hits the bedroom wall you can be sure
someone is naming a hurricane
and you are not immune.
Tonight, in some city, a criminal
will strike, but in Illinois
you are in everyone's living room
so why, passing through, does it surprise you so
to look past curtains, through lit glass
and see a young woman—
face blank as an angel's
bent before one man—
an altar,
pretending to be us all.

■ GALE RENEE WALDEN FROM *SAME BLUE CHEVY*

BRAIN ON ICE: THE EL TRAIN POEM

There's a seat right next to me
On the Milwaukee el,
Obviously vacant,
Awaiting some Loop-bound occupant.
Riders from Ukrainian Village,
Or maybe Warsaw,
Rush past me in righteous,
But ignorant horror.
Not calmed by my Givenchy tie
Or Bass boy penny loafers.
Apparently not reassured
By my literary look.
Unmoved by my perusal of the
New York Review of Books.
To them I am Cabrini Green
Strapped to an attaché case,
And for instilled fear
Of being robbed, stabbed, raped
Or worse
Conversed with incoherently,
They dare not sit next to me.

I am the Color Purple
In a navy blue overcoat.
I am Bigger Thomas on his way to work.
I may be Nat Turner on urbanized revolt.
I am Mandingo
With a big   thick   black
Toshiba laptop.
I am Super Fly with Oxford collar
And Harvard law degree.
An invisible do-rag hovers above
My missing Malcolm X shades,
There is a bulge in my pocket
And it might just be a blade.
I am the stereotypical cause-effect

That masochistically strikes them blind.
I am the charred rope with which
They hang their consciousness
During terrorized imprisonment
In Hollywood formatted blackness.

It is an undefiled seat
Adjacent to the door
Opening at the same Loop stall
Outside the deco-art marble plantation
In which we all
Are hourly enslaved.

■ MICHAEL WARR FROM *WE ARE ALL THE BLACK BOY*

A School Yard of Broken Dreams

They thought that the ball
would never stop bouncing,
stomping and jumping on the hot
grey gravel, like giant gladiators
ready for war

in beat up All Stars and stolen Nikes
gliding magically in the air, as if
a modern ballet set to urban funk

they were legends, but in their own
minds, there was Packin' Pete, Bustin' Billie,
Hooker Joe, Pockets, my home boy Sweet "T,"
and there was K-Town Karen, she was the only
girl that I'd ever seen do a 360 degree,
in yo' face, yo' mama do the nasty all night long
SLAM DUNK.

someone should've told them that there would
always be alternatives, that the cheering crowd
and cute azz, smooth-bottomed pom pom girls
were not life-long contracts
and that the yellowed newspaper clippings of their once
upon a time boyish and girlish grins
inside Bermuda shorts, accepting store-bought trophies
was not meant to last forever.

that the ex-loud mouth coach,
English teacher by day, co-owner of his old
man's restaurant by night, had alternatives.
No, the ball will never keep bouncing forever.

■ MARVIN TATE FROM *SCHOOLYARD OF BROKEN DREAMS*

EXPLODE

is the way i feel sometimes
but if buildings explode where do the people go
sometimes dreams explode
and you awaken cannon deaf, at least i have

chicago night is trash smoke, is lava steam
your sky could be crawling with women

■ MARY KATHLEEN HAWLEY FROM *DOUBLE TONGUES*

It's Not the Heat, It's the Stupidity

Red stick rendezvous, we ponder raft transportation
walking to the muck's edge, who can say if fourth
of July jolly-making pyrotechnics don't prevent
this city's wharf from turning into rusty cargo?

Skin n'bones sugarcane masters have become
the sophisticated sons of muffeletta excess,
keeping their long traditions of commerce, corruption
and kickbacks, allowing two-won barges to sail silently
with subtropical booty breaking the swamp's isolation,
bright as a Dog Star for Dixie deals and the Civil War.

On an overcast grey day, visitors
marvel at gnarled hulks of Mississippi
sassafras and shagbark hickory,
latched crab-like across metal beams and bridges,
the river is wide and blindly replenished, once
captive to gator lore and gamblers, today
it takes its liquids from simple shanty farmers
and millionaire pharmacists, still, no one white
recalls plantation fertility rites, songs of unconquered
slave night drummers, chawasha sisters and brothers,
muscles meshed in sweat, daylight branded on the back
and handed over for centuries beating past
mute liturgies laid down shoulder to shoulder,
under the sails of a jibe colossus sweeping the first
jazz piano player to cook rice and beans
for red stick's neighbor, New Orleans.

We are such frail witnesses
to an old baton rouge swollen with
blue laughter, unblinking black trains, and pier pilot flags
that flap for a commonwealth resplendent in its contradictions,
her industry's isthmus of aborted experiments encircle
the gulf's belly-filling crayfish for cajun connoisseurs who
may mock us, unaware of emergency-room reluctance,

no, they didn't feel Christ's conjured presence in
a bowl of tabasco-covered allergens when
hurricanes made our gumbo cooler.

■ CARLOS CUMPÍAN FROM *ARMADILLO CHARM*

TOMATOES

The poem draws from an account that appeared
in a California Central Valley newspaper.

When you bite
deep to the core
of a ripe, juicy tomato,
sing a psalm
for Margarito Lupercio,

Praise the 17 year existence
of an immigrant tomato picker.

But don't bother to look
for his fingerprints
on the thin tomato skins.

They are implanted
on the banks
of the Delta Mendota Canal,
imbedded on soft soil
where desperate fingers
grasped and pulled,
reaching out
to silent shadows on shore
as deadly jaws
of rushing water
pulled him to its belly.

Margarito had jumped in,
so he could keep working;
to escape,
      miserly taunts,
      stares of disdain;
      indignities of alienhood
to escape,
      Border Patrol officers tearing across
      a tomato field like cowboys,

to escape,
  the iron bars of desert cells
  and hunger's dried-up face.

A brother of the fields
heard Margarito's cries
as the Migra officers watched
and did nothing.

He tied together torn sheets,
shirts, loose rope –
anything he could find,
pleading for help
in the anxious tones
that overcome language barriers.

Officers, in your name,
watched
and did nothing.

Workers later found Margarito's body
wedged in the entrails
of a sluice gate.
They delivered it to town,
tomato capital of the world,
awakened now, suddenly,
to the tyranny of indifference.

■ LUIS J. RODRÍGUEZ FROM *POEMS ACROSS THE PAVEMENT*

ARMADILLO CHARM

I.

Armadillos are flattened on roads every week,
ending up like some cold drunk Indians
who lie down on warm dark asphalt after
trips back from fiery-watering holes.

Smart armadillos amble jobless,
happy not to work in a zoo, they stroll
plush river grass and smooth red pebble paths,
far from fast two-legged foreigners.

II.

Armadillos want to be around when the earth smears
the last mad zigzag road from her body,
armadillos are patient, armadillos count
every wind stir roaring off solar coasters,
bringing layers of fine star dandruff to land,
that's why they look like dried-up
sailors or the last face of thirsty travelers,
armadillos are prone to tropical leprosy,
like lost botanists they go skinning themselves
raw while roaming hungry in the dark.

Before the sky master tossed sparks to bake all creation
with telltale universal panther carbon, nothing big had died
yet, truly a nadir niche for four-legged fossils, though not too
bad for fishes, it nearly killed calorie-starved armadillo.

III.

Armadillo, ugly craggy creature, with twenty tribes
          across the hemisphere,
armadillo, with few friends from beginning to end:
the hairy tree sloth, and rapacious ant eater,
each claiming to be his pal, sharing a pre-Ice-Age pedigree
with the armored rascal, each sticking to the same survival
diet since making the Paleocene,

peg-tooth armadillo got hot under his sixty million year-old
scapular collar and became a cranium-hard tourist walking backwards—
going south to north, before entering borderland Texas.

Gringos discovered Armadillo in the mid-nineteenth century,
the indigenous people had always known him,
but history started with the newcomers ripe for independence,
Alamo insurance, Austin honky-tonks, accordion *conjunto*-polka suds,
salsa music, blue-eyed Baptists, plastic saints on dashboards,
chile-flavored beans and King Ranch cowboys trained by *vaqueros,*
raised on tacos of onion-soaked armadillo,
available only in south *Texaztlan,*
giving the chicken-colored meat cult status.

IV.
Armadillos are fond of colorful flowers, thorns pose no problem,
and armadillos love dark dirt body bugs, slugs and worms
on steamy leaves and bright powdery pistils-to-petals.
These are no obese armadillos.
Armadillo has no patent on this diet, so some of us
wanting to slim down just might like to try it. You go first.

Armadillo kitsch means being flayed for book ends, salt shakers or
decorative baskets to please some schmucks passing through airports,
armadillos become rustic *canastas* filled with pecans and
pomegranates after eyes are shredded by twenty-two caliber bullets,
there's no graveside music for their passing,
no lead-lined casket for a charade with eternity,
not a moment of ritual magic,
nothing cushions armadillo death when shells, cars or trucks
splatter red guts like gastral litter on subtropical scrublands.

V.
Armadillo prefers his original name in Nahuatl, *Ayotochtli,*
a combination of turtle and rabbit,
looking like a hedgehog in obsidian helmet,
sturdy enough to become an instrument,
complete with strings for *charanga*-mountain music,
Ayotochtli, Ayotochtli, Ayotochtli,

"Ah, don't touch me," he seems to say,
balling up after he burrows away
at speeds pushing fifty,
armadillos have lived like charmed moving stones
for generations, so don't knickknack them to extinction,
be compassionate compadres,
adopt one.

■ CARLOS CUMPÍAN FROM *ARMADILLO CHARM*

EL GRUPO MCDONALD'S

My father is seventy-seven and meets
with a group of "old timers"
every other day in a McDonald's
in the heart of Makati.
These men have worked
for the prestigious firms of Soriano,
Ayala, and Elizalde. Accountants,
Managing Vice-Presidents, District
Consultants, and Sales Representatives.
A white long-sleeved shirt, white trousers,
and a black leather belt is the dress code
for these retired *Ilustrados*.

The coffee is always hot and *los temas*
de conversación son, las bases Americanas,
el cambio del Dollar, la Cory Aquino,
y el tiempo distante cuando Manila
era la perla del oriente.
The city is changing color, fresh air
from the bay does not blow into Makati
and the pollution lingers all night.

My father tells me that Enrique,
the ex-Jai-alai star, died
over the summer, Ralph Zulueta is also dead.
He tells me that even if the group is shrinking
every year, they still talk about the idiots
in the government, the American bases,
the exchange rate of the Dollar, Cory Aquino,
and the days when Manila was still
the pearl of the orient.

■ NICK CARBÓ FROM *EL GRUPO MCDONALD'S*

VELVET

for Vaclav Havel

I can't tell you much, except
for the graceful aging,
the strength of history,
how young and hungry this city let me be.
If you don't know the language, you must
let your heart do all the talking.
If you don't know the language, it's easier
to believe what you hear.

I can't tell you much, except
how I cried the first time
I walked across the Charles Bridge.
The weight of it under my feet
lifting me up like a child
able to see it all in one breath.
My lungs filling with every
ancient hero, and the castle,
and the river thick and strong,
and the little old men fishing
or not fishing and the music,
gypsy born, teasing
the bottoms of my soul,
asking me to dance and
not taking no for an answer.
How all my definitions for beautiful
started scrambling for better words
in my head, and my American mouth,
awe-shaped and eager,
let the gulls fly in and out
searching for bits of bread
to fill their own.

I can't tell you much, except
how freedom felt here.
Frenzied and fresh,

newborn and nearly disastrous.
So much future to never regret again,
and every day a fantastic gift
from God, or someone
in an equally exalted position.

I can't tell you much, except
how the memory of revolution
hangs in the air like velvet.
And in every spot where
the absence of bullets made peace
scream through this city like fire,
the first furious flames burn bright
on their way to the green and
golden era of spring.

■ CIN SALACH FROM *LOOKING FOR A SOFT PLACE TO LAND*

2

AN ACHING

MOSAIC

within
it growls,
sometimes it sings,
it courses its way
and creates its own beauty...
EPT Dec., 1976

WE ARE A PEOPLE QUITE INTEGRAL

we are a people quite integral in being; it is our nature to
take pride in what we are—and though experience can hurt and
also cripple, we have survived and in so doing have created

> a sense of being-ness
> which flavors
> our speech patterns,

we sing—
we dance—
we shout—

to all our poetry,
our art reflects
the fusing of our languages,
we feel alive
whichever way we speak,
our words are thesis,
antithesis,
& synthesis,

we spiral forward
within our upward movement,
as we create
from praxis
a new language,

on that is vibrant, alive, and filled with pensive
strength.

■ Ricardo Sánchez from *The Loves of Ricardo*

FREEING THE FOSSIL

It is the language of words
and it is unlike anything
I have heard
with my fingers.
They are forming sounds
and in their stillness,
their eagerness shines
wide open and spilling
over everything
that is white or anything
that has been left alone too long.

They are telling me to dream
in colors I have not yet dreamed
and now
they are building me a house
to raise you in.
I had no idea they could be this gentle.
Their persistent prickling,
the stiff feathers that make my bed
so enduring.
They go on and on
and I wonder if they know me,
if they know where they are taking me,
and if they have been there before.

Together, we step carefully
through the unfinished bodies.
Translucent carcasses hold us in place
and eyes, or what once was,
stare up at me.
Memory, though I don't know whose,
makes them glisten with some kind of emotion
I have not yet touched.

Their stories have fertilized this ground
where the next step waits to fall,

and I raise to my lips this floor
of history's forest.
I lift it up to my mouth,
but before it can touch my tongue
for swallowing,
it sprouts wings.
It becomes the sky.

■ CIN SALACH FROM *LOOKING FOR A SOFT PLACE TO LAND*

SCATTERING DREAMS

Dear Mama, I am sitting
under the umbrella tree
with paper and pencil stub.
Since I have learned to write,
angels crowd my shoulders
like Missy's wedding shawl.

Mama, when I am writing
flight enters my bones.
I'm planning the note
for our crossing over to Jordan.
I suspect we will look into the river,
see our faces, see our hands,

wavering on the water,
even see our broad feet
and claim ourselves,
this body belongs to me,
these are my ample arms,
my knobby knees, my knotted hair.

Mama, I come here on Sundays at sunrise
practicing the plan. First, I write
my name, *Willa May,* then I write *Free.*
Then I seed my name.
I say *Willa May, Free* to leaves, to acorns,
to butterflies staring on the grass blades.

The soil under my heels start whispering,
nudging me to stand, walk, get moving.
Seems like I can't stay on the ground,
those angels swooping around my pencil
are the same ones fluttering about my knees,
scattering dreams everywhere.

■ ANGELA SHANNON FROM *SINGING THE BONES TOGETHER*

In An American Landscape

No ancestor of mine has sat between
these rows of corn in October under

the stiff tassels' white wind chimes. From the hard
kernels gone orange, the husks fall away

like money. Everywhere, it is a season of dry
vessels: wasps' nests hung like punch bags from

oaks, milkweed and mock cucumber gone to seed,
the latter like strings of white blowfish

rattling their mortality songs. A few maples
darken from the outside and glaze a burnt

orange shell the wind peels away. No words
will match the slow deepening and decline of

beauty on the roadside, or the way the sun
hits a yellow birch on the far side of

the marsh. A hawk flies up, settles on a fence
post. That would have been enough for my

ancestors: the moment of the hawk's flight,
the sideways glance at the blowfish husks where,

weeks ago, white flowers were—moments not
captured but imprinted in seventeen

syllables with nothing before, after, no
context about walking in the field and

returning to bread and soup, work, or love.

ii.

But I want the moment and its context, what
stretches beyond the brilliant
decline of maples. The seeds of a cattail

unravel and bare a stem like a burnt out
sparkler, From the fallen ocarina of a milkweed
husk, my breath blows out the notes left unplayed

by winds. I cannot sound the pure pitch of my
ancestors who left the seeds to scatter or
parch. Standing under the one maple left green,

its edges slowly yellowing in mid-
October, I imagine the light inside
an apple bathing me with knowledge. It is

not enough to utter one perfect note to
harmonize with the world's silence. I repeat
my broken phrases the way the wind gathers

and stirs the golden coins of poplars, spend-
thrift and miser both, counting what must be lost
to the silence spreading eastward with snow.

■ KYOKO MORI FROM *FALLOUT*

EXQUISITE MINORITY

When the stock market opened you could get
a really good steak dinner for three dollars—
one that would cost you sixty now.
Clout costs me: leg cramps, disc problems,
something around my heart they call dyspepsia.
I eat things bigger than I am but their brains are smaller.
Sheep, for instance, and cows.
In summer I pick mushrooms in France,
pay four hundred an ounce for the muskiest ones.
I like things that smell good—women,
barbecued beef. I once kissed a pig,
but I will not endure poverty.
As a child I chose the shoe in Monopoly.
I filled the Game of Life cars with pastel peg children
and went to jail then broke free. I got rich
on AT&T, Standard Oil. Mattel—
the best American in Englewood, New Jersey.
Most days, I'm nice to the maid
who irons my sheets just like my mom did.
I sweat in Armani, give me a break!
I'm realistic about money, power, taxes.
Of course, I'd like to be on TV.
I'd tell jokes to Letterman.
He'd laugh like a dad and invite me back.

■ DENISE DUHAMEL AND MAUREEN SEATON
FROM *EXQUISITE POLITICS*

GOOD TO HER

The Germans were good to her.
Giving potato peelings,
walking on softened heels.
And falling in love many times
with menless deaths,
she took on soldiers.

Rode her bike right to the front.

Gave up blood-sausage during
the war,
and traveled far in those five years.

Now, Sophie, enameled mirror and
a wide driveway in the suburbs,
the backyard willow outgains the yard.

To you, every wind means a mess.

Remember long candles in the night.
Sharp symbols carving beneath your dress.

Remember swans tense
as angels breaking glass
on Utrecht's ponds.

The smell too far off
of tallowed flesh and hooks
like mysteries
in the dark.

Dear Sophie, swollen with the war.
With the big German stock. Two-car garage.
When they first landed it was
scoops of fire dancing on the darkness.
The parachutes mauling what was left
of moonlight,

and fresh radish sandwiches,
and hymens in girls over
thirteen.
Or eleven.

Some were hung on crane hoists.
Some flickered in the fall
into chest-deep ovens.

And others now call
from their purring Plymouths.
The garage door falls
onto rakes
and lawnchairs
and swallows in dark

a most perfect neatness.

■ JEAN HOWARD FROM *DANCING IN YOUR MOTHER'S SKIN*

JEUNES FILLES

maison des esclaves, Senegal

probably here
in still blue silence
on smooth stone floors
always wet with tears

in the quarters for virgins
one hundred pound irons
petulance and death
attached to each shackle

while the clergy above
rest their elbows politely
on bleached bone interiors
drink the blood of christ
from crushed skulls and
torn flesh

our story lingers between
these dark rusted bars
plucked by human vultures
sifted through cold fingers
in this french factory of sorrow
sometimes whole families

papa to haunted tobacco fields
baby to bitter sugar mills
mama to endless magnolia stench
drowned in high cotton

■ ZADA JOHNSON FROM *MISSISSIPPI [R]EVOLUTIONS*

What I'm Telling You

If I say, my father was Betty Shabazz's lawyer, the poem can
go no further. I've given you the punchline. If you know
who she is, all you can think about is how and what you
want to know about me, about my father, about Malcolm,
especially in 1990 when he's all over t-shirts and medallions,
but what I'm telling you is that Mrs. Shabazz was a nice
lady to me, and I loved her name for the wrong reasons,
SHABAZZ! and what I remember is going to visit her
daughters in 1970 in a dark house with little furniture and
leaving with a candy necklace the daughters gave me, to
keep. Now that children see his name and call him Malcolm
Ten, and someone called her Mrs. Ex-es and they don't
really remember who he was or what he said or how he
smiled the way it happened when it did, and neither do I,
I think about how history is made more than what happened
and about a nice woman in a dark house filled with
daughters and candy, something dim and unspoken,
expectation.

■ Elizabeth Alexander from *Body of Life*

Of Fish

who knows the cold secrets of fish?
for whom do glassy eyes warm
with love?   to whom do fish sing,
evenings, mouths pumping small o's

from the water's lip?   breasts are fish
flopping like the day's catch
and hands are fish, pale claspings
birds are fish, knifing through clouds

in black schools, and so are pickles
packed with brine in the jar   beds
are fish, belly up after the night's
wild diving   who sees fish

dancing in storms, flanks shifting
with the beat of waves?   who tells the dramas
under ice, quick bleeding, hook pulsing
in each quiver of gills?   who knows

the names of fish, has seen their colors
miles underwater, and follows the last slow
spiral, the stiff drifting, blind eyes
open even as they are eaten?

■ Mary Kathleen Hawley from *Double Tongues*

Mt. Zion Baptist

Before Grandma couldn't walk,
we all went to church together sometimes.
We sat in one little group on the pew
like the pictures of black folk
on the back of the fans we used
to cool ourselves in church.
Mama wanted me to always do things
like they supposed to be done.
Her word for right was *businessfied.*
Even now when I am making love,
the woman gotta know I'm *businessfied.*
The singing was usually good,
and I knew all about this church.
I was in Sunday School and on
the Junior Usher Board.
I went to Baptist Training Union.
One Sunday in winter we went
to morning service, and I got bored.
I was getting to be fifteen,
feeling like a man, smelling my pee,
as Mama and her sisters called it.
So I put my hands behind my head
in church and closed my eyes.
I didn't want to hear that mess
the pastor was dragging out himself.
We went home and Mama told me
to go in the back room and take
my clothes off and get ready for a beating.
I took off everything except my underwear
and waited for her. She came in
like the roll of thunder and beat me.
I cried the cry of shame. I wanted Daddy
to come and save me. Mama had
gone stone crazy on my behind.
When she knew she was dying,
Mama apologized to me.
It was spring. I was thirty years old.

■ AFAA M. WEAVER FROM *TALISMAN*

Why Couldn't I Have Been Born A Baptist?

Senseless of harmony
We moaned our Druid-spawned version
Of a lifeless "Praise Jah" hymn.
In the hidden background,
Silent but loud, some heard
A higher being screaming:
"Can I give the drummer some?"
The funk sliding 'round the
Rims of our ears
Waiting to be rhythmned and bluesed
Away from a monotonous religious waltz.
Fantasizing 'bout being born a Baptist.
Swinging to the hallelujah palpitations
That reproduced rock n' roll.
If only one Saturday morning
She had not opened the front door
Letting them into our project home,
I might have been a Baptist.
Like she once was in New Orleans.
She remembered the fat black lady
In flowing white Sunday silk
So bloated with the Holy Spirit
She burst straight through the
Church door, not stoppin' runnin'
'Til she couldn't hear the
Bangin' of the gospel no mo'.
I wanted to be that fat black lady
With her hands swaying in the ether,
Eyes sealed, mouth open, and hair
Pointing back toward the pulpit as if
Pulled by the palm of the preacher's hand,
Trying to recapture her fat black soul
His processed "do" glowing with the
Power of Jesus and burning lye.

All I wanted was the woman's music.

■ MICHAEL WARR FROM *WE ARE ALL THE BLACK BOY*

I Am the Fourth Supreme

Spangle and wiggle,
Girl-child chic,
We're a backstreet Detroit upgrade:
clocking timepiece moves.
Hear us and you say "girl"
with three R's and a honey slide
That's what Mr. Gordy says.

A few bars into us
and little girls run for brush mikes
and bounce along to a rough-boy beat.
We're the baby love tasty enough
for general sensibilities,
not just the less profitable homie market
That's what Berry says.

But Diana,
A drop-eyed shark smile behind four-foot lash,
Diana's pushing front lines,
Diana's pushing shine,
Diana's pushing Berry.

But we push on.
Back beat in a negative arrangement,
black matter on an all-white image,
backing away from an ethnic roar
as the silver gathers.

■ LISA BUSCANI FROM *JANGLE*

PUBLIC RADIO PLAYS EDDIE HARRIS

Clouds stand in protest of morning.

I wonder should I cross this picket-line sky and go to work.

The 70 bus stood me up for our 8:32am date.

Headlines say I voted for a man who cheated on his wife.

By 2:00pm my body's at war with a virus.

I am now blue fire.

My throat is lined with cactus.

There was no mention of this in the morning paper.

I crawl back home to my room; my bedsheets are cold.

At 10:00pm a call of bad news from my family:

Something about a car and my brother.

Doctors say he many never dance again.

This chord of bad news accompanies today's riff.

Folks *have* gone on strike in heaven.

Sweat pours off the shoulders of the night.

No need for liquids and drugs, I'm already dead.

If WPFW FM can't resurrect me, Lazarus was a liar.

Thank God, they're playing Eddie Harris.

I have friends who are atheists.

I have ammunition for our next argument:

They play four Eddie Harris tunes in a row!

Faith healers are tuning in.

I'm all but cured when they make the announcement:

Eddie Harris died today.

Thoughts tornado over my bed.

It pirouettes over the city with hips like my mama's.

Eddie always said there's no such thing as a wrong note,

Only bad connections to the next.

I put the alarm clock under the sheets.

In the morning it will sound like music.

■ A. VAN JORDAN FROM *RISE*

DERRICK POEM (THE LOST WORLD)

I take my $, buy a pair of very bright kicks for the game
at the bottom of the hill on Tuesday w/ Tone who averages
19.4 points a game, & told me about this spot, & this salesman
w/ gold ringed fingers fitting a $100 dollar NBA *Air Avenger*
over the white part of me—my sock, my heel & sole,
though I tell him Avengers are too flashy & buy blue & white
Air Flights w/ the dough I was suppose to use to pay the
light bill & worse, use the change to buy an Ella
Fitzgerald CD at *Jerry's*, then take them both in a bag
past salesmen & pedestrians to the C where there is a girl
I'd marry if I was a Pablo Neruda & after 3, 4 blocks, I spill out
humming "April in Paris" while a lady w/ a 12 inch cigar
calls the driver a facist cuz he won't let her smoke on the bus
& skinny Derrick rolls up in a borrowed Pontiac w/ room
for me, my kicks & Ella on his way to see *The Lost World*
alone & though I think the title could mean something else,
I give him some skin & remember the last time I saw him
I was in the B-ball court after dark w/ a white girl
who'd borrowed my shorts & the only other person out
was Derrick throwing a *Spalding* at the crooked rim
no one usually shoots at while I tried not to look his way
& thought how we used to talk about black women
& desire & how I was betraying him then creeping out
after sundown with a girl in my shorts & white skin
that slept around me the 5 or 6 weeks before she got tired
of late night hoop lessons & hiding out in my crib
there at the top of the hill Derrick drove up still talking,
not about black girls, but dinosaurs which if I was listening
could have been talk about loneliness, but I wasn't,
even when he said, "We should go to the movies sometimes,"
& stopped.

■ TERRANCE HAYES FROM *MUSCULAR MUSIC*

NOTES FOR A POEM ON BEING ASIAN AMERICAN

As a child, I was a fussy eater
and I would separate the yolk from the egg white
as I now try to sort out what is Asian
in me from what is American—
the east from the west, the dreamer from the dream.
But countries are not
like eggs—except in the fragileness
of their shells—and eggs resemble countries
only in that when you crack one open and look inside,
you know even less than when you started.

And so I crack open the egg,
and this is what I see:
two moments from my past that strike me
as being uniquely Asian American.

In the first, I'm walking down Michigan Avenue
one day—a man comes up to me out of the blue and says:
"I just wanted to tell you...I was on the plane that
bombed Hiroshima. And I just wanted you to know that
what we did was for the good of everyone." And it
seems as if he's asking for my forgiveness. It's 1983,
there's a sale on Marimekko sheets at the Crate &
Barrel, it's a beautiful summer day and I'm talking to
a man I've never seen before and will probably never
see again. His statement has no connection to me—
and has every connection in the world. But it's not
for me to forgive him. He must forgive himself.
"It must have been a very difficult decision to do what
you did," I say and I mention the sale on Marimekko
sheets across the street, comforters, and how the
pillowcases have the pattern of wheat printed on them,
and how some nights if you hold them before an open
window to the breeze, they might seem like flags —
like someone surrendering after a great while, or
celebrating, or simply cooling themselves in the summer
breeze as best they can.

In the second moment — I'm in a taxi and the Iranian
Cabdriver looking into the rearview mirror notices my
Asian eyes, those almond shapes, reflected in the glass
and says, "Can you really tell the difference between
a Chinese and a Japanese?"

And I look at his 3rd World face, his photo I.D. pinned
to the dashboard like a medal, and I think of the eggs
we try to separate, the miles from home he is and the
minutes from home I am, and I want to say: "I think
it's more important to find the similarities between
people than the differences." But instead I simply
look into the mirror, into his beautiful 3rd World
eyes, and say, "Mr. Cabdriver, I can barely tell the
difference between you and me."

■ DWIGHT OKITA FROM *CROSSING WITH THE LIGHT*

WELCOME

When I was little and brown
The humming plane stopped
Midway Field was there
And I was proud of my blue shorts
White shirt
Blue socks
White shoes
True Puerto
Rican proud.
Excited by Colgate smiles
Like the ads nailed
To my town's walls.
So I was confused
And shivered
When the December
Chicago wind
Slapped my face.

■ DAVID HERNÁNDEZ FROM *ROOFTOP PIPER*

3

MADE FROM

GHOSTS

TWO DAUGHTERS

At the table we pass bread, salt,
>thin slips of butter, little plastic dishes
of chopped tomato and onion
>to drop in the salad. My father cranks pepper
into his soup, my mother folds her napkin,
>my sister sips from a cracked brown glass.
Nobody speaks, and nobody eats, under the table the
>dog's legbone thunks the tile.
And then the odd part of every night where the wall clock ticks
>and we fall into the sound, high white cliffs
from which tiny tacks sprinkle. The door doesn't open, I watch
>the knob stay still, occupying exactly one space, a brass globe
shiny as the tiny country of somewhere-else-that-is-not-here.
>I count to ten anyway, gamble away math grades,
>Christmas presents,
our beach trip in August. My father clears his throat,
>rubs his eyes, and I almost say *He's not coming,*
how much longer will you pretend he might be coming?
>But suddenly I'm older, I know something about kindness,
my will drops away like a heavy locket breaking from my neck. I bend
>my head to eat even while my eye watches the door's
>brass button
stay the same, not-twisting with his not-touch.
>Months continue to pass like this,
years tumble after quickly. We keep working at safety
>while my brother's chair at the table fills
with jackets, books, umbrellas, fills and fills
>until we remember that he'd never been born.

■ JOSIE RANEY FROM *AMERICAN VIGNETTE*

MISCARRY

To glimpse herself in the mirror might have meaning,
she's not sure what. She won't turn on the light.
The faucet spits. She works the bitter soap
into her skin, wrists, abdomen, her throat;
and her breasts lift. She twists her dripping hair,
absorbed, methodical, alone, she won't
turn on the light. Here touch is different—
for once it asks for nothing.

                                        There were four,
hairless, mouthless, unbreathing, nameless, who
could call them children? She remembers, though,
each will, the dogged fastening to life,
even when she guessed that she would lose them,
and wished, dreading the wish, that her tight womb
would relax and give...the way, in the end, it gave.

She knows them now, lost things. She knows herself
contained in the black glass, containing absence.
And this—it must be instinct—all this washing.

■ ANNE-MARIE CUSAC FROM *THE MEAN DAYS*

POEM FOR THE UNNAMED

They say if you don't
name a child when it is born,
it will start crawling north,
unable to be pulled back
by the string of its name.
It will start the party
without you, without names.

Once on a busy downtown street,
I saw a woman lower
a blue rope around her
two children saying:
"This is for safety.
Because I love you"—
and she pulled the knot closed.
A perfect lasso of love.
And so her children went
in blue orbit around her,
and so wherever they wandered
she could pull them back
by the string of their names.

Or perhaps they had
no names. And so
she bound them tight
with ropes, afraid they
would go spinning away from her,
without names,
without ropes,
away.

■ DWIGHT OKITA FROM *CROSSING WITH THE LIGHT*

I TAKE ALL MY TROUBLES

I take all my troubles
I stack them up on a shelf
I take all my troubles
I stack them up on a shelf

I am
a girl so blue and lonesome
I gotta carry my blues
all by myself

When the mid
wife carved me from
your fate
bound my reaches
for you mother

and I can remember
no cries
for your absences

I did
not though ever
want to know
your lovers
benign or cruel

I did
not though ever
want to know step
daddies or their up
bringings' expectations
of me

A male
child imagines
his mother

and you stole
part of my fantasy

I got
so many troubles
I send half to school
I got
so many troubles
I send half to school

Ain't much
else to do
when down and out
the golden rule

■ Sterling D. Plumpp from *Blues Narratives*

Blues for My Daddy

1.

what does it mean
when Ogun is standing
behind you in the
grocery line

greenville face
beneath a white
hard hat

just like your
old man the time
when he came
in, thumb bloody
and broken

sent home half
a day with a
prescription
for pain

but says the most
outstanding pain
is building a world
for other people's
children
to enjoy

2.

functional love, I
suppose, is nice
work if you can
get it

like a concrete
job on michigan
or a foreman's
position up
north

but for the rest
of us it is fixed on
repaired daily

breaks down and
leaves us stranded
on empty shoulders
although I have read
the letters you left us
in whiskey ink

I still imagine
that you are the son
of a mississippi
god

a tragic hero song
harmonized by gladys
knight, backed up by
the pips

a tangible
fallible man
worthy of a little
girl's love

■ ZADA JOHNSON FROM *MISSISSIPPI [R]EVOLUTIONS*

FATHERS

I see the lattice of my father's face
in the mirror—lines from the bridge of his nose
run under my checks; my forehead
creases above his watery eyes and droopy lids.
I scratch, laugh, and trace my
scaffolding with his gestures.
I can't hide his carpentry in my features.

You say your father played the same music,
printed with my hand, built life out
of hard work and the poetry of Roosevelt Road.
I wish I could be him—loved by the song
in your eyes when you speak of his quick turns,
read right even when I do wrong.

I tried so hard not to grow the way
my father was built. He would have demeaned
yours, rejected the music, laughed at
the printing, and ignored whatever it said.
I wanted to write him off for adoption,
just the way he took me in.

Like your father I loved the blues, booze
and ladies, yet felt my father's hatred
grown large and bitter like some choking
weed breaking down the trellis of love
we're born with in our hearts—my love
crumbled, my face a penance, myself a father.

■ MICHAEL R. BROWN FROM *FALLING WALLENDAS*

ON THE FOURTH OF JULY...

excerpt from Bum Town

I lie on a blanket
And the sky rips open
With fire
And white tendrils
Of hope.
My Dad lights
His cigar with a
Road flare
And tells me
About Okinawa—
Tracers and bullets,
Sailors and marines—
When he thought
Every night was
Independence Day.
Only to wake up
The next morning
And see bodies strewn
On the beach,
Mile after whistling mile.
Marines and sailors
Felt the sea
Roll and swell
Under their legs.
Lengthening shadows
Mocked them from
The deck of the
U.S.S. Noble.
My Dad and every other
19-year old
On this ship
Wanted only to be beyond
The bloodshed,
The blank, dead faces.
Our guys,

Their guys,
In the blood and sand
He couldn't tell one
From another.
My Dad looked up
At the rockets,
A red one burst
Around his head
Like a nimbus
Of bloody light
And his shadow
Falls across my face
Like a shroud
Made from ghosts.

■ TONY FITZPATRICK FROM *BUM TOWN*

THE KILLING FLOOR

That morning inside the Swift packing house
we went on the killing floor together,
grey smoky light and cold air in winter.
You pointed out meat hooks, crank and conveyor belt,
sick with stoic manhood that weighed on you
like a blood-mark from that frozen room.

Sawdust swept down and powdered your face
as I twitched across an elevated platform.
Stranded below me, you seemed small, childlike,
looking up from the narrow tier abutted
by a tilting rail. I watched you, father,
withdrawing from everything outside you.

The roof shivered like a spine, pinching
the hollow above me as you passed from sight,
a slim moonbeam in the dark below.
A cold draft descended. Something else
floated down, moon-white, filial, silent,
and followed you to the tank house

dragging a carcass skewered with knives.
I called to it. Then it too passed,
the cross-marked fire door closing shut behind,
and the hollow of my voice
deep and knotty over the haunted floor.
I was no longer your fine child

but a bone or mineral in another body.
Throughout that dark place I heard
one door after another swing shut,
and you, moving outside, ask something
swallowed by the chaos of the wind,
then climbed down after the ringing silence
to cross over with you into this life.

■ ANDRES RODRÍGUEZ FROM *NIGHT SONG*

GUTTERS

Fall Saturdays my father called me
down to the carport for the season's ritual chores,

we changed spark plugs, wiped and stacked the pegboard's tools,
and once a year climbed a ladder tilted to the roof

to free the gutters from leaves. My father would tie
a rope around his waist, then mine, tug-testing it twice,

and balanced by his steady counter-weight I would crawl
on my knees to the ledge, gouge out solid married leaves and sticks,

fling them to the ground where my mother's kerchiefed head
bobbed over roses, my sister spread pinestraw under the Japanese maple.

A lazy girl, I hated this chore above all others,
loathed how at night while undressing

I'd find a few spots at the hip where the skin had peeled back
under the rope's burn in a mark of my attachment.

If I had believed then what I half-believe now,
that everything we do is a gentle metaphor,

with every handful I would have cleared the closing paths
of my father's heart, and might have saved his life.

Those fast seasons on the roof I tripped just once,
my father lunging a few steps forward,

yanked by a weight that must have surprised him,
must have seemed to have grown overnight into the full

and real girl of me. I snapped my head up in time
to see the worried *o* folding creases up his face,

on my way down, a fall of full years before I understood
what catches and who holds.

■ JOSIE RANEY FROM *AMERICAN VIGNETTE*

DISORGANIZATION

My doctor tells me the new hitch in my heartbeat is inexplicable,
but it disturbs my sleep
and is connected to that slight cough when I am tired.
Not to be confused with the old hitch in my heartbeat
from most of the seventies spent on speed,
or that other slight cough
from thirty years of pipe smoking and fat cigars.

My father echoed his father:
it's not the growing old that bothers me
but the falling apart that goes with it.
They broke down like old factories,
their machinery chocked and shimmed
to tolerances no caulking could pad,
their dynamos gone eccentric,
powering down,
their foundations shattered by vibrations.
Dust and gunk clogged the sump pumps and generators
until their tattered roofs collapsed,
their doors flapped in least wind,
and they were defenseless against the rain.

This is not a sympathy plea.
You will understand that when it happens to you.
I only come out on days when I feel all right.
I stay home when my blood feels like oatmeal,
my lungs like wet sponges,
my head like the clouds east of some industrial town,
my prick of whithered stopcock
dripping hot acid down a tin leg.

On days like that it's enough to make a man
scrape together transit fare to step in front of the train.
But the tough old guys go for the good days as long as they can,
even though they see the world through weepy eyes,
resent their limbs for their fundamental unyielding awkwardness,
hate their teeth because they will outlast them.

There's no shame in growing old,
but don't you young people try to tell us how hard life is.
We may hear a certain world-weariness in your voices,
but we feel it deep in our bones.

■ MICHAEL R. BROWN FROM *FALLING WALLENDAS*

TURNING FORTY IN THE 90'S

April 1990

We promised to grow old together, our dream
since years ago when we began
to celebrate our common tenderness
and touch. So here we are:

Dry, ashy skin, falling hair, losing breath
at the top of stairs, forgetting things.
Vials of Septra and AZT line the bedroom dresser
like a boy's toy army poised for attack—
your red, my blue, and the casualties are real.

Now the dimming in your man's eyes and mine.
Our bones ache as the muscles dissolve,
exposing the fragile gates of ribs, our last defense.
And we calculate pensions and premiums.
You are not yet forty-five, and I
not yet forty, but neither of us for long.

No Senior discounts here, so we clip coupons
like squirrels in late November, foraging
each remaining month or week, day or hour.
We hold together against the throb and jab
of yet another bone from out of nowhere poking through.
You grip the walker and I hobble with a cane.
Two witnesses for our bent generation.

■ MELVIN DIXON FROM *LOVE'S INSTRUMENTS*

TRACE

out of habit,
I often remove
my shoes and leave

them by the side
of the bed, socks
rolled up into

the cavern of each
shoe—left there,
that simple. One

afternoon Alex,
the five year old,
runs into the kitchen

to inform her mother
that the bedroom "stinks"
of Daddy's feet.

I am cooking pasta
and I cannot contain
my laughter. She pinches

her nose. I've been singled
out for my scent, and she,
she will remember

something about my
having been there
and here.

■Virgil Suárez from *You Come Singing*

THE DEAD STILL WALK...

excerpt from Bum Town

This city.
I dreamt once that
Children burnt in a fire,
With only their arms for blankets,
Sang in the frozen night
Outside a church
While angels wept down upon them.
92 children howled and screamed
Like dying animals,
Singing for God
To let them
Back in.

The dead still talk
In this city.
My Dad drove an ambulance
For Thompson Funeral Parlor
At 79th and Ellis
And sometimes the dead
Spoke to him through
The radio
Or called him on the phone
But when he turned
On the TV
They'd only
Stare back
Waving silently
In black and white.

The Irish dead still talk
A lot in this city.
The fog is like cigar smoke
At the foot of the lake,
And Richard J. Daley
Could always see through
The smoke.
Every wink, every nod,

Every smirk
Turned into highways,
Skyscrapers and bridges.
"I'm a kid from the stockyards—
I'll stand with you."
And he did.

Then the Irish
Licked the frosting,
Ate the cake
And sold the
Plate.

Who built the pyramids?
Mayor Daley built the pyramids.

■TONY FITZPATRICK FROM *BUM TOWN*

LETTER FROM FOREIGN

Dear Mum, there are so many things I have
to tell 'bout 'Merica, the place where you said
the streets are gold and there are many people
with good hair (like those in the movies).

'Member when I use to play with the toy helicopter
and fly away a foreign? Well, Mum, Dearest Grand Mamaa,
I have news for you. 'Merica is not in the sky
like the planes but is on land, flat land, droopy corn-fields
and choking chimneys, with latrines, and doo-doo
and frowsy ragamuffins as good as dead on sidewalks.

Mum, you tell me say God bless America for the people
here good, I have some more news for you.
Sure, some people go to church and chapel
and mosque and synagogue and march and pray
and some smile when they see you on the street
(some don't say 'Morning, dog' and sometimes
them cross the street when we pass them—
for an healthy Black man is a dinosaur
blowing fire at the people with pretty hair
and you know how easy it is for hair to catch fire.)

Mum, you tell me that they have scholarships galore.
And, a true. But you never say anything 'bout glass,
'bout aquarium and how buckra can encase you
in glass so that no matter how loud you scream
no matter how much you bark, the ceiling still there.

I don't want to bring down God on me so I must say
that education here good and that we learn all kinds
of things 'bout Greece and Rome, me speak Italian
now, some French—even Japanese. All these things
that you wanted me to do, Mum, but there is lots of glass about,
lenses, ceilings, bottles and they're all trained on me, you know,
reflecting, watching, waiting and laughing,
but I have to follow your lead, almost a century
and still not weary yet, I must never get weary yet.

■ ROHAN B PRESTON FROM *DREAMS IN SOY SAUCE*

THE MONSTER

It erupted into our lives:
Two guys in jeans shoved it
through the door —
heaving & grunting & biting lower lips.

A large industrial sewing machine.
We called it "the monster."

It came on a winter's day,
rented out of mother's pay.
Once in the living room
the walls seemed to cave in around it.

Black footsteps to our door
brought heaps of cloth for Mama to sew.
Noises of war burst out of the living room.
Rafters rattled. Floors farted —
the radio going into static
each time the needle ripped into fabric.

Many nights I'd get up from bed,
wander squinty-eyed down a hallway
and peer through a dust-covered blanket
to where Mama and the monster
did nightly battle.

I could see Mama through the yellow haze
of a single light bulb.
She, slouched over the machine.
Her eyes almost closed.
Her hair in disheveled braids;

each stitch binding her life
to scraps of cloth.

■ LUIS J. RODRÍGUEZ FROM *POEMS ACROSS THE PAVEMENT*

BATTLE

It has been eight months
since I've looked into the toilet bowl
and seen my reflection spitting up all that is good in me
piercing my thorax with bitten nubs
blunted by years of acid reflux
index and middle worked so consistently
they now host incomplete ovals
where my identity seeped out one meal at a time.

In my locker I kept the books
no one thought it would occur to me to read.
In my house I kept score of who was winning the war,
my mother or me.
You'd think she would've noticed the cover up
water running, leftovers left on the plate
but she was busy reclaiming her body
putting on pounds he had denied her for years
it was fear that kept her bird boned and emptied.

In Psych 101 they say it is a white girl's disease
brought on by years of exposure to Vogue
sour lilies on a waif mother's vanity
a tea party of sunken skeletons
working their way through skin with gossip and tweezers
and maybe it was the white girl in me wishing her away to the front
through the layers of hip and sway
to the front where college recruiters could see her
all blonde and lean and shake her hand
without fear of contamination.

And maybe it is the white girl who is lonely now
that there are no ulcers guarding her burden
lost she wanders the mountain ranges of my body
wondering when I let go
but I know better
this battle is old habit
one like any other racist twitch
and it lives in the repetition of unloving everything we are
starving all cells equally until you become something other than yourself.

■ ARIEL ROBELLO FROM *My Sweet Unconditional*

HOMECOMING

To the city storefronts locked
with black metal gates and iron bars,

to the five a.m. sweeper that slips past
over dirty streets, plastic bags

stuck to light poles ripping overhead in the wind.
This first hour, a false dawn,

as I walk head bowed to the pavement,
snowflakes catching fire in headlights

slicing the air. I'm home, again,
into quiet, lighted waters.

I see not the distance crossed but the shorter
middle ground, a space in and around

my parents' home, vibrating
with some new old message there.

On the porch, I feel the flooring sag
under the weight of years

knocking me off balance,
my keyless hand gripping the icy doorknob.

I stand awash in the morning's ghostly light
till I see my mother's shape moving

behind the glass, descending the stair
like I've seen a thousand times from inside.

Now outside, it saves me from the fall
into eternal wintry dark.

She opens the door, her arms,
a warm sweep of air behind her.

I hug her small shoulders, patting
the sweat-damp nape of her neck.

"I rode all night to see you."
She pulls at my long hair and turns,

quietly stepping into the dark of the house.
"Your father had a feeling you might come."

Lighting the stove, she's lit by pale flames,
her face a photograph of something past

but not forgotten, her words
a song pulling me out of the shadows.

And in our sight we recognize each other,
as if for the first time,

mother and son, unknown lovers,
repeating mysteries of faith.

■ ANDRES RODRÍGUEZ FROM *NIGHT SONG*

Hearing about the Mystery Lights on a Bus near Joplin

It's gorgeous in this southwest corner of Missouri.
The orange trees in autumn
and the *spooklights*
if you're there on the road at the right time of night.

When you first tell me about the strange lights
that appear on some dirt road
I think they're large as haywagons.
But they're small, you say.
You can almost hold them in your hand
as though lanterns carried between farmhouse and outhouse.
Or someone walking to the barn.
Or going to the chicken coop
to see if it's closed for the night.
The lights always moving, you say.
The way dead bugs on the windshield
could still be said to fly.

■ DIANE GLANCY FROM *THE RELIEF OF AMERICA*

PRETENDING THE GHOST

Every Sunday morning,
I wondered what it was
that made my mother
rumble.

Was it the Rev. Matthew Thomas,
72 years of spirit in his spine
propelling him across the pulpit
like hot air popcorn?
Was it the way his bended body
stiffened with the message,
God's wagging finger
swelling his throat with howling,
or the veins in his head bulging in time
with the choir's doo wop rhythm?

Was it the gut songs of the devout,
who truly, truly believed,
women with hats like satin ski slopes
and men with Saturday night's whiskey
still steaming from their pores?

I'd sit there, perfect in pink anklets and pigtails,
praying to the 3-D cardboard Christ
to please not let my mother embarrass me.
But sure enough,
when the Rev spit the right wail in her direction
(accompanied by a hop, skip and jump
his body was clearly incapable of),
I saw my mother's toes curl.

Her eyes would roll back into her head,
her face would twist,
and I couldn't help thinking
that she looked constipated instead of possessed.
Someone would whisk me away,

and when I came back
her stockings would be down around her ankles,
her eyeglasses would be cracked,
and for the rest of the service
she'd be rocking like the Temptations
and whispering in some alien tongue.
My mother no more, my mother still.

Later she'd say, "Just the spirit got in me, chile,
that's all."
Couldn't figure out why the spirit wasn't gettin' in me too.

So two weeks later,
I kicked,
screamed,
slapped two deacons,
showed my best underwear to the congregation,
lost my favorite hair ribbons,
three buttons
and a front tooth.

My mother wept, clearly overwhelmed
at my performance
and God's entrance into my 6-year-old soul.
God, however,
gazing at me from a blacklight version
of the Last Supper,
clearly could not take a joke.

It was at that moment he condemned me to a life
of sloppy kisses from men with post-nasal drip,
a life ruled by the fake father,
the pseudo son,
and the phony ghost.

■ PATRICIA SMITH FROM *LIFE ACCORDING TO MOTOWN*

COUGH MEDICINE

Grape Robitussen tastes like melted lollipop.
It sits by my bed, heroin melting in a spoon.
I want it. I want the grape. I want to sleep.

Already in school they have had us read books
where the junkie goes cold turkey, shakes and shivers
on a cot. I am an opium-eater

who swigs from the bottle, falls into swollen sleep.
I ride the **HORSE**. I have a **MONKEY** on my back.
Already I am the kind of child who should not

be allowed to read so much or late at night.
But now I am coughing like the consumptives
in my books, match-girls black from chimney dust,

and if I cough I cannot sleep; if I don't sleep
I cannot dream of all I'm reading: bony fingers
that snap off and turn to candy, children who slip

down the bathtub drain, who are frozen in place forever.

■ ELIZABETH ALEXANDER FROM *BODY OF LIFE*

THOUGHTS OF AN AMBIVALENT CARNIVORE

I could be vegetarian.
It would probably work for a while.
But what good would it do,
except for my health
and my psyche?

Non-violence can only go so far.

Would I have to stop swatting mosquitoes?
Spraying roaches?
Stepping on ants?

Even Jesus was a fisherman.

Animals kill animals,
without any training from us.

Maybe there was a garden of Eden,
where lions and lambs played harmlessly,
and rabbits snuggled up with dogs.

But every animal goes for food,
where nature tells him to find it.

Christians eat the Body of Christ;
lovers nibble each other;
baby sucks mother's breasts.

We kill one another with kindness.

The old give way to the young;
I'll have to move over.
But please, move me gently.
Don't be in a hurry;
hesitate.

Let me savor these last few
burgers and dogs.

■ JOHN SHEEHAN FROM *LEAVING GARY*

4

BENEATH
THE CLATTER

NIGHT TRAIN

She boards the car in a manner not quite fierce,
not a challenge, either, though one long-haired man
moves quickly from the doorway. Tall, her large
face emerging from the night outside,
she steadies two paper-handled shopping bags,
a bundled infant, and clasps the hand
of the young child who hesitates behind her,
clutching her dress, his face and unsaid "No!"
as she hoists him to the seat beside me; settles
the baby and herself across the aisle.
In the departing lurch she grabs a bottle,
begins to feed, and in turn fed by
her infant's rhythmic and insistent swallowing;
his face, intent with pleasure, eyes half-closed;
or something else, perhaps the left hand
patting the bottleneck, or the right one
which opens slowly, slowly makes a fist;
she glances briefly, rarely across the aisle,
not seeing the other climb into my lap.
Until he has. She looks up, again looks down,
her eyes empty of anger or approval.
He smells of milk and talc and sits a moment,
his cornrowed head just below my chin,
then pulls himself to the glass, seeing the lights,
points at a distant building, pulls my hair,
and slaps his palm against the window, laughing
until he is tired and, suddenly, asleep.
I look up. Across the aisle his mother
sleeps too, still hugs the infant close to her,
nodding over it. I look back down—
his body slack and deeply, heavily warm,
face buried in my folded cardigan,
his breath unheard beneath the clatter, noise
of brakes, the nearby voices as we move
tonight, together, deep into the city.

■ ANNE-MARIE CUSAC FROM *THE MEAN DAYS*

Insomnia in N.Y.C.

For Christina

"...the night, has a thousand dialects."
—Lady Blue

I am happy
to have her home
again, her eyes are filled
with tired excitement.
I do not ask of her, how was her night
or what stranger she has seen
she'll discuss this, after the harsh
outcries of our next door neighbor
as he watches in anguish, the TV shooting
of his favorite hero, Marshall Dillon.

And so we sit, listening
To the white noise of the ceiling fan
spinning endlessly into oblivion
the junkie mother pacing the dimly
lit hallway, in search of her imaginary
daughter and Peter, the crazy ex-con
turned artist, trying to convince the
night clerk into allowing him to paint
murals in all of the ugly lilac colored
rooms, in exchange, he shall have his
room for free.

slowly she peels herself out of her blue
sequin dress, while lying on the bed, as
if a mermaid washed ashore into the hands
of the peasant fisherman; I've prepared for
her, a tub of warm water in which she
washes away the smoke and finger prints
of faceless johns...she reenters the tiny
room, I tell her how our neighbor screamed
so loud that he stopped would be thieves
in their tracks after contemplating a
robbery; she gives a reassuring smile

and gently pulls the covers over her
beautiful body, while somewhere in the
night, the sax player fills her dreams
with noise, lots of white noise.

■ MARVIN TATE FROM *SCHOOLYARD OF BROKEN DREAMS*

Daybreak Wakes

Daybreak wakes
my pains in the morning
Sunset reads
to my hurts
at night

Daybreak wakes
my pains in the morning
Sunset reads
to my hurts
at night

Worry
Worry

all the time
no matter
if it's in the dark
or in the light

I got
this liberated anger
under house
arrest in my songs

And I know
it is no "Magnificat"

a black girl sings a
cross Mississippi hills
mud and red
clay choruses
throbbing with blisters

hoes dish
water and low
down men bring

And I can
not say a rosary
for you since
the only beads
you know

are knots
side your head
and columned
on your spirit

My dreams
just little birds
jumping from trees
to die

My dreams
just little birds
jumping from trees
to die

Got
no pretty colored
feathers on their wings
to make them fit
to fly

■ STERLING D. PLUMPP FROM *BLUES NARRATIVES*

EATING IN ANGER

My friend lived with a man who ate
peanut butter when they fought. She
found the spoons in his pockets, sticky
inverted mirrors in which her angry
words blurred backwards, out of
order, the way he might remember
years later in the middle of some
sleepless night. Once, in his suit-
coat, he left the plastic wrap
for Oscar Mayer's bologna he'd
eaten sitting in his car—bland
pink meat stuffed into his mouth
like false tongues, paper-thin.
                              I'm not much
for eating in anger. In my last
fight, I took a pot of rice just
cooked and dumped it in the sink for
the god of domestic rage who
lurks in drains or underfoot
between the fibers of a dirty
carpet where another woman might
toss the casserole out of her
dish. The spoon I flung hit
the poster of Van Gogh's *Irises* and
cracked the glass over the leaves—green
candles weeping molten wax.
                              There's no
end to my hunger for vindication or
vindictiveness though later I wish
to eat my words the way people
devour cars for the Guinness Book of
Records; they sip tires and steering wheels
cooked into black paste or soup. If
I could lift the spoon from the floor
to scoop out the ground glass over
the broken shafted irises, if

I could swallow my anger and turn
spotless as washed glass, believe me
I would—I would open my mouth
in joy.

■ KYOKO MORI FROM *FALLOUT*

WHEN THE NEIGHBORS FIGHT

The trumpet's mouth is apology.
　　We sit listening

To *Kind of Blue*. Miles Davis
　　Beat his wife. It hurts

To know the music is better
　　Than him. The wall

Is damaged skin. Tears can purify
　　The heart. Even the soft

Kiss can bite. Miles Davis beat
　　His wife. It's muffled

In the jazz, the struggle
　　With good & bad. The wall

Is damaged skin. The horn knows
　　A serious fear.

Your tongue burns pushing
　　Into my ear. Miles Davis

Beat his wife. No one called
　　The cops until the music

Stopped. The heart is a muted
　　Horn. The horn is a bleeding

Wife. Our neighbors are a score
　　Of danger. You open

My shirt like doors you want
　　To enter. I am tender

As regret. Mouth on the nipple
　　Above my heart.

There is the good pain
　　Of your bite.

■ Terrance Hayes from *Muscular Music*

HALLOWEEN

Tonight we can be anybody we want:
a woman says she's entropy
but nobody gets it; a lobster pulls
a card from the deck with his claw.
It matches the one in my hand. Outside,
a werewolf screams into the pay phone
then deposits more coins. A while ago,

a passive aggressive divorced a narcissist
with manic tendencies. Their daughter
showed signs of regression so the court
assigned her a lawyer. There are tests
designed to unmask our maladjustments,
personality bents, significant elevations
on the not-in-the-child's-best-interest scale.
The court-ordered psychologist told me
denial would not be tolerated
in his sessions. I looked back, listening
to the air conditioner kick on, then off.

I wish it were five years from now.
Then it is. I see my daughter and ex-wife
like binary stars, bright, cheerful
and a billion miles away. In the lobby
an alien samples the quiche, he talks
about the building's footprint. A cool
breeze from the open window stops me—
the sweet scent of fallen leaves and rain.
It is a difficult joy that rises out of grief.
A crow caws along with the music, then stops.
In another room a man pulls off
his goat's head, a woman tears up her face.

■ MIKE PUICAN FROM *30 SECONDS*

Boy Sneezes, Head Explodes

Inspired by a headline in a super-market tabloid

There are no pictures with this story,
strange when one considers the possibilities.

There could be a pre-sneeze montage,
dim photos of a boy being bounced
on his father's knee,
a terse 8th grade graduation shot,
or something taken at Boy Scout camp
four years ago.
Any shot with his head still
attached to his shoulders
would pretty much get the point across.

Or afterward, man-on-the-street candids
of surprised passersby
showered with bits of gray matter,
shards of nostril,
clumps of hair,
ragged shreds of facial tissue.

The tabloids could run
full color action shots
of the poor guy's torso
teetering back and forth
doing that crazy circumstance dance
and finally falling,
flopping on the sidewalk
like an orgasmic guppy.

The electronic media would be sure
to pick up the audio
as some witness jerk
mumbles "gesundheit"
or even worse
"God bless you."

But I guess
anything in the way of illustration

would either be too early
or too late.
Who could see the pinpoint of irritation
growing insistent like a hot white light in his head?
Who could follow that errant bit of dust
driven deep by the wind?
How could he know, when he opened his mouth,
that once he closed it
it wouldn't be there?

■ PATRICIA SMITH FROM *LIFE ACCORDING TO MOTOWN*

TO BE HEARD

for Cindy Salach

It will always be like this.

When we finally fit the key
and unlocked cages of words,
when we began to fashion the phrases
that chained our burdens to the world,
when we were chosen the cup
of some creative divinity's grace,
we knew we were on to something.

We cut and buffed every facet of life
for the crowds to wear as they wished,
offered hands filled with the fat fruit
of our imaginations.
We skated on straight lines
that reached the point faster
than modern geometry would allow.

And the drink they filled our lips with
quenched us in its wash.
"I liked it,
you made me cry."
Poets don't live on this libation alone,
but let me tell you,
it goes really well with a burger.

And now that's our milk.
And quite frankly,
it's never known a better mother.

And that's why it hurts
when we're pushed back to the way it was:
when we face the tight, dark places
where the light doesn't catch like it should;
when all the perfect pictures spin out of our mouths
like clouds

and disseminate;
when our patience is smacked and laughed at;
when our voices are thrown back
like vicious spit balls;
when the air in our lungs is mopped up and wrung out.
And we know
that beyond all the progress we'll ever make
somewhere,
sometime,
it will always be like this.

Someone will always cut us with dismissal,
and begin to rebuild the walls
that we tore away
to enable us to do this in the first place.

But film to film,
trace to trace,
the scar tissue thickens
around our hearts
and braces them for breaking.
Rip and heal,
tear and heal.
And what once made us bleed profusely
dries as soon as it rises.

It will always be like this.
But what we leave in trying
is the legacy of
Effort.
And that's a very sweet word.

Scream on.
Next time
it won't hurt so much.

■ LISA BUSCANI FROM *JANGLE*

ANG TUNAY NA LALAKI RECEIVES INSTRUCTIONS FOR HIS LAST WORKSHOP POEM

for Fiona Templeton

You will need pen and a piece of paper.

1

You will go up the stairs into St. Mark's Place,
Go up to a stranger and ask him/her to give you one word.
Example: "Hi, I'm writing a poem and I was wondering
if you could spare a word, any word that comes to mind."
(Don't forget to thank the stranger.)
You will write that word down as number 1.

2

You will walk up to the intersection of Lafayette
and St. Mark's (Astor Place). You will stand
next to the giant cube metal sculpture on the middle
traffic island and you will listen
for a specific sound—an onomatopoetic sound.
Example: Grrrrr-ting, grrrrrrrrrrr-ting, grrrrrrrrrr
of a jack hammer pounding on asphalt.
(Stand there at least ten minutes, filter out
the first three obvious sounds. Listen
for the subtle sounds of a plastic bag blowing by,
the wheels of a baby stroller, the scrape
of a leather shoe made in Italy.)
You will write that sound down as number 2.

3

You will walk to the Barnes & Noble book store
on Broadway and St. Mark's. You will enter
the store and go up the escalator or elevator or stairs
to the second floor Poetry Section. You will choose
a book of poems from the many shelves.
You will open the book to the second poem
and you will read the first line of that poem.
You will write down that line.
(Don't forget to put the book back after
you note the author of the poem and the title.)
You will write that line down as number 3.

4

You will walk back to the Astor Place subway
entrance (the uptown side). You will go down
the stairs and stand near the exit turnstiles.
You will look for the expression on the face
of the first person to exit from the train.
Example: Gruff, solemn, elated, kind, needy.
(No need to interact with individual.)
You will write that expression down as number 4.

5

You will walk back to the workshop at 37 St. Mark's Place.
Along the way, you will catch the momentary scent
Of something in the air. You will look for
and identify the source of the scent.
Example: Pizza, bus exhaust, a woman's perfume,
urine on the sidewalk, rotting garbage.
(Don't frighten the female pedestrians by trying
to smell their hair as they walk by.)
You will write the scent down as number 5.

6

You will come back to this table and decide
whether to begin writing the poem for the remainder
of the class time or go home to write it over the weekend.
You will write a poem with six stanzas,
each stanza will have six lines of varying lengths.
In the first stanza you will begin the poem with the word
in #1, you will also use that word in the sixth stanza.
In the second stanza you will incorporate
the sound, #2, in any of the six lines.
In the third stanza you will use
the first line from the book, #3, for the last line
of the stanza and the last lines in each of the six stanzas.
In the fourth stanza you will place the expression
of that face, #4, in any of the six lines.
In the fifth stanza you will put the scent,
#5, in any of the six lines.
In the sixth stanza you will use the word in #1
Anywhere in lines 2 and 4.
(Good luck.)

■ NICK CARBÓ FROM *SECRET ASIAN MAN*

AUTOMATIC WRITING

The writing hand doesn't distinguish
between fiction and observation.
-E. Kostova

It's a rush at the page, a way to break up
the sediment. I write furiously
with the tapping foot, the bleeding cuticles,
the slow asthmatic breath. Suddenly I'm
at Walgreen's. Behind the counter
pharmacists are blowing up plastic gloves;
they're trained to make you wait
15 minutes. I stare at the glass, poorly
digest my lunch. Words spill out and surround me
like relatives at a smorgasbord
who point to my plate and ask for a bite, like
strangers who just appeared on my couch
as you listed all your concerns
about our relationship. These uninvited guests:
they arise out of nothing. The man calls
another name, then disappears into the shelves.
I hear the faint shuffle of pills, the quick inhalation
of someone who's about to speak,
then doesn't, the sound of your shoes
against linoleum leaving my apartment,
tires squealing from your car
exiting the parking lot. Someone writing
all this down. We start out not knowing
where it leads, then we read it—like walking
through a door into a small room,
then into a smaller room after that. Call it art
based on something ending.

■ MIKE PIUCAN FROM *30 SECONDS*

"CONVICTS, INMATES
& FELONS, TOO..."

convicts, inmates & felons, too,
behind those shuffling feet
and vagueness in the eye
exist worlds yet to be explored;

mine and tap those hidden reservoirs,
flower, my friends, and blossom forth,
let the pen
guided by your fervent minds in quest
lead you onwards
to those quiviras of joyful life;

create coyote realizations and
let your city blues eviscerate,
undulate toward those spheres
where the mind can garner
meaning and loving happenstances;
the word is mighty
when it portends
a way of life which sanguinely
sings of joy and freedom,
and freedom is a responsible
existential praxis
which implicates us
in our mutual development.

in knowing you
I sing you
songs of what it can mean
to travel worlds
and to celebrate
so write and live,

for time shall pass,
but more importantly
you shall walk those streets,

but walk them proudly/creatively
and in love
with all that life can mean to you...

gracias for everything
brothers in prison blues.

From "lemon Creek Gold:
Panning for a future—
An Introduction of Sorts"

■ RICARDO SÁNCHEZ FROM *THE LOVES OF RICARDO*

THE LIFESTORY OF EDDIE JAMES "SON" HOUSE JR. AS TOLD THROUGH HIS HANDS

In the fields, she touched me with dew-moist hands.
She was the earth lifted in my blue hands.

A man must live to have a life to sing.
He dies to have ashes lifted by hands.

Are there no limits to a bluesman's life?
Cotton & guitars: Picked by the same hands.

A train's whistle holds possibilities
Much like the backsides or the palms of hands.

In the audience, there are more blue eyes
Than I can recall my hometown had black hands.

If you think these are wrinkles in my face,
Come, hear my life story told through my hands.

A preacher is nothing but a bluesman.
Bible? Guitar? All the same in my hands.

A workday is so long, the hours immense.
But my grip! Look at the size of these hands.

Your spirit becomes your eyes in prison.
Who questions a spirit with two strong hands.

Evie, with workdays as large as your eyes,
No one strums blues from my bones like your hands.

■ A. VAN JORDAN FROM *RISE*

LITTLE GIRLS, 1993

The night I went to the play
and you waited on our steps,
I imagined you a little girl.
Somewhere in the fifties
on your steps on Spruce,
playing. It hurt me to see
you so innocent, as you can be
so innocent sometimes, and
here I was in the wilderness
of my own past, called out
of the wedding oath to slay
my dragon. My heart was broke,
broke and broken and overfilled
with itself. I cannot
make you see how one day
I awoke and had to follow
this need to break away.
I was in a cab coming home
late to the house you hated,
this brick assemblage built
seventy years ago. You hate it,
and I have since given it to you,
as it is the last material thing
I can give. I can't blame you.
I can only blame me for not striking
out against the way people come
to love me, despite my need to be
in the lonely room in East Baltimore
where I grew up. In a full house,
alone. I have to go back there
and find the *talisman* that has
made me a prisoner of love,
against the wishes of my dreams
at night, all gone in the bones.

■ AFAA M. WEAVER FROM *TALISMAN*

DANCING IN YOUR MOTHER'S SKIN

for Ed Gein

Ed, you've been a naughty boy.
But who can tell what
darkness swims between
a young boy
and his mother?
Your little hands snug
as a cockle
around her fingers
now are claws
that dip right in.
An oceaned viscera
glistens in the wind
of the backyard shed.

Poor little Ed.
The hulk of your mother
on your back.
I, too, am ashamed to let
her near,
but crawl into her skin
at my every fear.

A gutless course we've taken here.
Moonlight trailing on the backporch screen.
Don't let me into
the heart that starts up after
midnight.
Don't let me sing
a vacant lullaby
with the buzz saw.

The line is thin
between a boy and all
the close-calls
that make him real.

Washing off the night's ink,
the bed is only a half-room
away.
But let it reel in its
pallid valor
for the moon is just right,
and you're dancing in your
mother's skin.

■ JEAN HOWARD FROM *DANCING IN YOUR MOTHER'S SKIN*

SPRING CLEANING

First goes floordust, then newspapers
stacked near the bed. Peanut shells
swept out of hiding between mattress
and rug. Toenails clipped.
Sprouts of a beard shaved off.
With hourly glasses of Deer Park Water
and the barest of food, the body
sheds winter fat and filler.

The hair goes next, close
to the gleaming, gleaming skull.
You are ready for the sun
and the salt-tongued air.

You are someone new. I will be
someone new, like you, and promise
not to hear the rattle our bones make
moving from empty closets
and all through the room.

■ MELVIN DIXON FROM *LOVE'S INSTRUMENTS*

Appendix: Study Questions

Questions for Section 1:
The Stars and Stripes Stripped

Pledge of America

■ How does the title interact with the content of the poem? Is this poem designed to be sarcastic? If so give specific examples.

■ Who are "the Pow Wowists?" What is their position in American history?

■ Describe specific images within the poem that correspond with question #2.

In a Tar-Mangled Manner

■ This poem is a parody of a famous song. Identify the song.

■ Once you have identified the song, give direct examples of words within In a Tar- Mangled Manner that are metaphors to the original song.

■ Explain the line "the charred fruit is still there."

■ Write a poem using this same technique using a song that references United States history.

Workers

■ Are the themes in this poem universal or are they only experienced by Latino families?

■ How does the narrator view his parents?

■ What doesn't the narrator want from life?

■ Write a poem about the difference between the way your parents see the world and the way you see the world?

First Day

■ What event does this poem document?

■ How does the narrator feel about this event?

■ Who are the people involved in this event and how do they feel about this experience?

JFK for a Day: The Tour

■ What historical event is being recreated by the tour? How do you know this?

■ Is this a tour you would like to take? Explain why or why not.

Marquette Park, 1966

■ How does the narrator of the poem portray her neighborhood in the first stanza? Based on her description, how does the community feel to you?

■ Given the date of the poem, to whom is the narrator referring to when the word *King* is mentioned? Why is this particularly significant?

■ Explain the line, "my father was thirty-two and handsome/and the clerical collar he wore/propped him up higher than the rest of us."

■ What do the "Butcher, Baker, Locksmith, and Thief" have in common?

■ Explain in a single paragraph how and why the neighborhood changed as the narrator begins to tell her story.

■ What kind of human characteristics are displayed by the neighborhood people in the poem?

■ Explain the line, "None of us really went home again..."

Song for the Nineties

■ Give two examples of contrasting images of ethnicity, religion and nationality.

■ Explain the conflict between the Tutsi and the Hutu. What movie portrayed these two ethnic groups in conflict?

■ Explain what the author is attempting to say with the couplet, "Beware of the devil who lies inside/your brother, your sister, yourself."

■ Write a paragraph explaining the couplet, "Beware of talking with any of these/but beware the more if there is no talk."

■ Write a poem using historical context contrasting things perceived as "good" and "evil." The poem should be written in couplets.

Exquisite Politics

■ According to the narrator of this poem, describe the "perfect voter" in terms of human characteristics.

■ This poem is an exquisite corpse. That means that two or more people passed the poem around and wrote a predetermined amount of lines in response to the lines written before them. How does knowing this help you understand the dynamics of the poem?

■ What is the overall meaning of this poem? Are there any metaphors in this poem? If so, what do they mean?

■ According to the narrator of this poem is America really the home of the free and brave?

■ *Politics* (noun) and *politic* (verb) both appear in the poem. What is the difference in the meaning of the two uses?

■ What are the speakers saying about the nature of politics?

Rave Politics

■ Politics has many different denotations (meanings). How is it used here?

■ How does the title of the poem explain its cadence?

■ Look at the word trail in line 19. What is the significance of the way it appears on the page?

Everyone's Living Room

■ What kind of image comes to mind when you read the line, "In houses wrapped/with porches, rocking chairs are wearing treads/in wood as people remember the first time?"

■ Who is the young woman in the poem bent before? Why is she doing this?

■ Describe in one paragraph what the author means by the title, "Everyone's Living Room," and how do the images resolve the meaning of the poem.

Brain on Ice: The El Train Poem

■ What is the main theme of this poem?

■ The narrator is careful to describe his attire. What kind of effect does this have on the people who have entered the train?

■ Given the thematic intention of the poem, what would be your best interpretation of someone headed "Loop-bound?"

■ Where and what is Cabrini Green? Explain the lines, "to them I am Cabrini Green/Strapped to an attaché case."

■ In the second stanza of the poem, the author mentions names like Bigger Thomas and Nat Turner. Who are these historical figures and how do they relate to the overall theme of the poem?

■ Give a complete synopsis of the poem in two paragraphs. Use specific examples to support each point.

■ Write a poem describing a personal experience similar to the one in this poem. The poem should be written in tercets.

A School Yard of Broken Dreams

■ What does being a "legend in their own mind" mean in reference to the characters of this poem?

■ How does the term "yellowed newspaper" impact the significance of the poem?

■ What is the overall theme of the poem?

■ Describe in one paragraph the meaning of the phrase "the ball will never keep bouncing forever."

explode

■ The narrator uses the poem "explode" to express different emotions. There are at least three examples of the narrator doing this. Identify those three examples and elaborate how explode is used as a metaphor in each example.

■ In the second stanza of the poem, the city of Chicago is referenced. Explain how this reference relates to the entirety of the poem.

■ What is the significance of women in the poem?

It's Not the Heat, It's the Stupidity

■ List some of the images that indicate the geographical location of this poem.

■ Given the specificity of region in this poem, discuss in two or three sentences the meaning of the phrases: "plantation fertility right," "songs of unconquered slave night drummers," and "daylight branded on the back and handed over for centuries."

■ Discuss the placement of Christ within the poem? What is the overall meaning of the poem and to what group of people is this poem focused?

Tomatoes

■ In four sentences, sum up the major points of the story in this narrative poem.

■ Does the narrator tell you what is the right or wrong way to think about this subject?

■ Why did the other workers bring the body of Margarito Lupercio to town?

■ Will you be able to look at tomatoes or any of the food you eat in the same way knowing how the people who pick them for you are treated?

Armadillo Charm

■ In part two of this poem, what exactly is the author attempting to say in the second stanza?

■ Referencing the title, what is the charm of the Armadillo?

■ Who are the Gringos in this poem?

■ Who are the indigenous people?

■ Is the author attempting to use the armadillo as a metaphor? If so, what does the metaphor represent?

■ Why does the author encourage the reader to adopt an armadillo?

El Grupo McDonalds

■ What role does the use of Spanish play in the poem? How does the poet resolve any issues concerning its use for non-Spanish speaking readers?

■ What lines in the poem reveal the social class make-up of those meeting at the McDonald's in Makati?

■ How is the saying, "the more things change, the more they stay the same," reflected in the poem?

Velvet

■ What kind of experience is the narrator of this poem having in the re-telling of this moment?

■ Judging from the language of this poem is this experience an epiphany? Explain why or why not.

■ What kind of transition has the setting undergone?

■ What kind of mental picture comes to mind when you hear the phrase, "the memory of revolution/hangs in the air like velvet?"

■ This poem describes the political climate of Prague, Czechoslovakia following a major change in government, led in part by Vaclav Havel. Research Havel or other leaders of political movements and write a poem describing the events of that movement.

QUESTIONS FOR SECTION 2: AN ACHING MOSAIC

We Are a People Quite Integral

■ What is different about the look of this poem?

■ How do the line breaks affect the way you read the poem?

■ Who is the "we" to whom the narrator is speaking?

Freeing the Fossil

■ How does the narrator feel about words?

■ What do words do to the narrator?

■ Where do the words the narrator wants to consume end up?

Scattering Dreams

■ What is the relationship between this poem and "We Are a People Quite Integral" and "Freeing the Fossil?"

■ To whom is the narrator speaking?

■ At what point in history does this poem take place?

■ What plan is the narrator practicing?

■ Write a poem about what you would do if the right to write were taken away from you.

In An American Landscape

■ What are the differences between the first and second sections of the poem?

■ Where and why does the poem reference haiku?

■ If the haiku form focuses on a natural scene in a moment in time then what does the author want now that she is "in an American landscape"?

■ How does the mention of "silence spreading eastward" make you feel?

Exquisite Minority

■ This poem is an exquisite corpse. That means that two or more people passed the poem around and wrote a predetermined amount of lines in response to the lines written before them. Start a line of poetry and pass it on to a friend. Make the poem no longer than 24 lines. See if a theme comes up. See if it works best to name it before writing or after.

■ What is the mood of the poem?

Good to Her

■ What is the time frame of this poem?

■ What is the significance of candles in this poem?

■ How does the narrator feel about the way in which these survivors are living now?

jeunes filles

■ What type of place is being describe?

■ When is the poem set?

■ When did the actions described in the poem happen?

What I'm Telling You

■ This poem is full of historical information. List the bits of information the narrator has written to tell you in this poem.

■ How does the narrator feel about the commercialization of El Haj Malik Shabazz (Malcolm X)?

■ What do you feel is the most important bit of information in this poem?

Of Fish

■ These fish are metaphors. Identify what the fish represent.

■ Is it good that we know so little about so many people in the world?

■ Why is the last image of a fish being eaten with its eyes open?

■ Write a paragraph using an animal as a metaphor for people in your school. Make sure you know enough about the animal to write how they look, smell, feel, taste, sound. Relate your knowledge of the animal to the way you feel about the people in your school.

Mt. Zion Baptist

■ What is the language of the poem?

■ Does anything in this poem remind you of a time in your life?

■ Do you feel that the mother should have apologized to the narrator of the poem?

Why Couldn't I Have Been Born a Baptist?

■ Compare and contrast the views of the narrator of this poem to those of the narrator of "Mt. Zion Baptist."

■ What are the music references in the poem?

■ From the first line of the poem there are double meanings to words and images. List the lines that have multiple meanings and provide two examples.

I Am the Fourth Supreme

■ Who were the Supremes?

■ Is there an all women singing group who resemble the women in this poem?

■ Write a poem in the voice of a modern singer as if they were thinking of other singers who are currently popular.

Public Radio Plays Eddie Harris

■ What is the effect of making each line a stanza?

■ What does it mean to have your "body at war with a virus".

■ How does the narrator react when he's told about his brother? How does this differ from the way he reacts when he learns Eddie Harris died?

■ Who was Lazarus and what is his significance in the poem?

Derrick Poem (The Lost World)

■ After reading the poem once, scan it again. What do you find interesting about the way the poem is written?

■ How does the narrator feel about decisions he has made?

■ Is the narrator comfortable with the friends from his younger days?

■ Who has changed more, the narrator or Derrick?

■ *The Lost World* is metaphor. What does it represent?

Notes for a Poem on Being Asian American

■ Culture is passed on through art, language, and food. In the first and second stanzas what does the narrator use to symbolize the way he feels about being Asian in America?

■ The first story the narrator tells is of his interaction with whom? What do the sheets that are on sale have to do with the story?

■ The second story sets the narrator in a taxi with an Iranian cabdriver. What does this story lead us to know about the way the narrator views cultural differences?

Welcome

■ How does the shape of the poem give you a clue to the political leanings of the narrator?

■ Is the weather mentioned in this poem a metaphor? Identify.

■ Relate the images and feelings in this poem to those expressed in "Notes for a Poem on Being Asian American."

QUESTIONS FOR SECTION 3: MADE FROM GHOSTS

Two Daughters

■ Give a brief paragraph description of how the narrator uses time as an extended metaphor. How many time shifts are in the poem?

■ What is the significance of the title? How does it relate the last line of the poem?

■ Explain the line "he's not coming." Who is the speaker in this poem?

Miscarry

- Why does the narrator wash herself the way she does?

- Who are the beings the narrator cannot forget?

- How does the narrator feel about her loss? Does she feel sad or conflicted? Use lines from the poem to substantiate your answer.

- How do you feel about the narrator by the end of the poem?

Poem for the Unnamed

- In the narrator's culture what is the ritual for babies and why?

- What does the narrator wonder when he sees a woman with her children tethered to her?

- Write a poem about your name. Include in the poem what you like about your name and/or don't like about your name.

I take all my troubles

- What kind of traditional Southern form does the first stanza of this poem represent?

- Identify the voice in which the first two stanzas are written.

- How can a person carry blues by themselves? Give specific examples.

- What is a mid-wife? Does this give the poem a timeline?

- Explain the line "When the mid/wife carved me from/your fate."

- What kind of sentiment does the narrator have for his mother? Give specific examples.

Blues for My Daddy

- Ogun is the god of metal and war in the Yoruba religion. How does this image resonate in the image of the first three lines and what is its significance?

- Explain the line, "building a world/for other people's/children/to enjoy."

- In section two of the poem, the narrator refers to love as functional. What is meant by this? Is this love a verb or a noun?

- Who is the "you" in the poem? What is "whiskey ink?"

■ What is meant by the term "tragic hero" in relation to "you" and the overall theme of the poem?

Fathers

■ Identify the physical features you share with your family members?

■ How does the narrator feel about his father?

■ How does the narrator feel about the father of whom the poem is addressed?

■ What does the narrator finally realize about his father and himself?

On the Fourth of July...

■ What immediately comes to mind when you read the term. "the sky rips open/With fire/And white tendrils?" Is this image an effective way to begin the poem? Why or why not?

■ Was the narrator's Father a Japanese or American seaman?

■ There is reference to age in the poem. What is the relevancy of age and does this have a psychological effect on the narrator's father? Why or why not?

The Killing Floor

■ Did you know that this is the method for the way meat is processed?

■ How does knowing this make you appreciate the work that must take place before meat is delivered to the grocery store?

■ Is the narrator speaking of an actual event, a dream, or using this scene for some other reason?

Gutters

■ In what ways is this poem a metaphor for life?

■ What is the significance of the image of father and daughter tied to the rope on a roof?

■ Why is it important to understand who catches and who holds in a parent-child relationship?

Disorganization

■ How does the narrator use factory machinery to explain the physical and mental health of his father and grandfather?

- List the images of the poem that affect you the most in the poem.

- Is there a clear and vivid image of suicide in this poem? If so, give the specific example.

- What is the message to the younger generation?

- Discuss how the title intersects with the body of the poem? Why do you think it is called *Disorganization?*

Turning Forty in the 90's

- Who is the speaker in this poem? Is he or she talking to a spouse or a loved one? Who is the oldest?

- What are some of the gripping images that hint at growing old?

- Why does the speaker use the image of a walker and a cane? Does the title fit the poem?

- Research and discuss the drugs named in the poem. What illness do these drugs combat? Discuss how the poem makes you feel.

Trace

- The narrator reveals one of his quirks in the beginning of the poem. How do you feel about his quirk by the end of the poem?

- What are the family dynamics in this poem?

The Dead Still Walk...

- The speaker uses many references to the dead. How are the dead used as metaphor throughout this poem?

- What is the influence of the dead on the living? Go through each stanza and give specific examples of death affecting life.

- How is the term "pyramids" used in this poem? How did Mayor Daley build them and what do the last two lines in the poem suggest?

Letter from Foreign

- Where is the narrator when he is writing this letter?

- What does the narrator want the receiver of the letter to know about where he is?

- Have you ever gone somewhere that you thought was going to be wonderful but once you were there you were greatly disappointed? Write about that time and what you learned about expectation.

The Monster

■ Why does the narrator of the poem refer to the sewing machine as "the monster?"

■ What do you think was the main purpose of this sewing machine? How did it impact the child's life given the images used in this poem?

■ Write a poem in quatrains describing something about one of your family members who make daily sacrifices.

Battle

■ Judging from the language in this poem, from what type of disease does the narrator suffer?

■ Referencing the poem, what are some of the general and physical characteristics of this disease?

■ Explain the line, "index and middle finger worked so consistently."

■ How does the mental condition of the mother and her marriage consequently affect that of her daughter?

■ What role does *Vogue* play in the deterioration of the daughter?

■ How do the daily images in the media play a role in the mental stability of the narrator?

■ What is the ethnicity of the narrator? Give specific examples within the poem to substantiate your conclusion.

Homecoming

■ Identify the poetic form in which this poem is written? Why do you think the author chose this form?

■ There are several images used by the narrator to describe the time of day. List the ones you think are most effective and substantiate your choices.

■ What do you think is the personal relationship between the narrator and the mother?

■ Explain the line, "repeating mysteries of faith."

Hearing about the Mystery Lights on a Bus near Joplin

■ What are "*spooklights*" and why does the author italicize this word?

- Does the narrator provide clues as to what the *"spooklights"* represent?

- Explain the line, "The way dead bugs on the windshield/could still be said to fly."

Pretending the Ghost

- What is the narrator curious about regarding her mother's behavior in church?

- What are the images the narrator uses to describe the minister?

- Identify the narrator's punishment for "pretending the ghost"?

Cough Medicine

- The narrator compares cough medicine to what addictive narcotic?

- Where does she get the idea to compare them?

- What are the similarities and the differences between the two?

Thoughts of an Ambivalent Carnivore

- How does non-violence relate to being a vegetarian?

- What are the significance of growing old and the idea of vegetarianism?

- How does the narrator use the idea of vegetarianism as a metaphor?

- In what stanza does the poem shift to provide the reader clarity regarding the poem's meaning?

- Write a poem about your teenage years using an animal as metaphor.

QUESTIONS FOR SECTION 4: BENEATH THE CLATTER

Night Train

- What are the demographics of the people in the poem?

- How does the speaker in the poem feel about the woman and her children? (hostile, happy, hopeful, ashamed, etc...)

- Does the speaker in the poem know what the mother is thinking or feeling?

■ When you look around on buses or trains do you observe the actions of people? Do you usually place a story onto the people you see? Write a poem about a person or people interacting with each other on the bus, train or in a crowded public space.

Insomnia in N.Y.C

■ What are the ideas put forth in each stanza?

■ What is the relationship between the speaker and the woman in the poem?

■ Describe the kind of place in which the people in the poem are living?

How does ethnicity exhibit itself in the poem?

Daybreak Wakes

■ The poem begins with a blues song. What are the elements of the blues in the song and the poem?

■ What images does "liberated anger under house arrest" bring to mind?

■ How does the closing blues song relate to the opening blues song?

■ Do the blues songs add to your understanding of the poem? Why or why not?

■ Is an understanding of the ethnicity or culture of the poet necessary to understanding the poem?

Eating in Anger

■ What examples of eating does the author provide?

■ Who are the people in the poem?

■ What could the bologna that is eaten by the man in the first stanza symbolize?

■ Study the stanza breaks. What is interesting about them?

■ How does the author now handle her anger?

■ What ultimately does the author wish to do with her anger?

When the Neighbors Fight

■ How does the poem look on the page? In what ways does the large amount of white space affect your reading the poem?

- What lines are repeated? How do their meanings change because of repetition?

- How does the narrator of the poem use music to speak about his personal relationships?

Halloween

- Most people associate Halloween with children. How does this poem reveal the relationship between Halloween and adults?

- Where does the narrator of the poem go in the second stanza of the poem?

- People are dressed in different costumes. Describe the types of conversations they are having in their assumed personas?

- How does the author feel when he is confronted with the smells of fall outside the window?

- Are their any images that feel absurd to you?

Boy Sneezes, Head Explodes

- Where does the author find her inspiration for the poem?

- Does this poem seem absurd?

- What are the larger issues discussed in the poem?

- Pick up a tabloid in a super-market and see if you can write about an absurd claim or story. Can you make us feel for the plight of the person or people in the article?

To Be Heard

- How does the narrator feel about words?

- What are the extended metaphors she uses to make words seem like more than words?

- The narrator says, "'I liked it, you made me cry.' Poets don't live on this libation alone." What are the other things poets need to live?

- The seventh stanza that begins "Someone will always cut us with dismissal" – what is the extended metaphor and what does it mean?

- Write a poem full of metaphors about whatever it is you like to do and how people treat those who do what it is you like to do.

Ang Tunay Na Lalaki Receives Instructions for His Last Workshop Poem

■ What is the form of this poem?

■ Try to write a poem in the way that the poem instructs.

Automatic Writing

■ How does the epigraph (the opening quote of a poem) prepare you for the poem?

■ How does the poet relate the events of the day to the problems he's having in his relationship?

■ Choose a day to make notes of the things that happen to you and then add in some of the ongoing drama in your drama as it pops into your mind.

Convicts, Inmates & Felons, Too...

■ What segment of society is the narrator addressing?

■ What does the narrator want his audience to do with the "worlds yet to be explored" by the audience.

■ What do you feel the narrator hopes for the reader by the end of the poem?

The Life Story of Eddie James "Son" House, Jr. as Told Through His Hands

■ The author of this poem studied the life of Eddie James "Son" House, Jr. What are the particular pieces of information you think he had to look up to include in the poem?

■ This poetic form in which this poem is written is called ghazal.

a. How many lines are there in each stanza? How does the first line of the first stanza end? How does the second line of the first stanza end? Identify the word that concludes every stanza.

b. What does the narrator mean when he says "In the audience, there are more blue eyes/Than ...my hometown had black hands?"

c. What is the mood of the poem?

d. What do you think Evie's relationship is to the narrator?

Little Girls, 1993

- How does the narrator feel about his former wife?

- What is the internal conflict of the narrator?

- Why does the narrator give his wife a house she hated?

- What is a *talisman* and why does the narrator feel he needs one?

- Does culture or ethnicity play an important role in the poem?

Dancing in Your Mother's Skin

- To whom is this poem addressed?

- What are the images of family in this poem?

- How do you feel about the people in the poem?

Spring Cleaning

- This is a list of the things the narrator is cleaning for spring. Identify those things the narrator "cleans?"

- What does spring symbolize in the poem?

- How is spring contrasted with the health of the narrator and the person who is the object of the poem?

TIA CHUCHA PRESS BOOKS, ANTHOLOGIES AND CDs 1989-2005

Poems across the Pavement
by Luis J. Rodríguez
ISBN 0-9624287-0-1

We Are all the Black Boy
by Michael Warr
ISBN 0-9624287-1-X

Life According to Motown
by Patricia Smith
ISBN 0-9624287-2-8

Rooftop Piper
by David Hernández
ISBN 0-9624287-3-6

Stray Bullets: A Celebration of Chicago
Saloon Poetry,
edited by Ida Therese Jablanovec,
Susen James and Jose Chávez
ISBN 0-9624287-4-4

Dancing in Your Mother's Skin
by Jean Howard, photography
by Alice Q. Hargrave
ISBN 0-9624287-6-0

Dreams in Soy Sauce
by Rohan B Preston
ISBN 0-9624287-7-9

Jangle
by Lisa Buscani
ISBN 0-9624287-8-7

Crossing with the Light
by Dwight Okita
ISBN 0-9624287-9-5

Double Tongues
by Mary Kathleen Hawley
ISBN 1-882688-00-7

Open Fist: Anthology of Young
Illinois Poets
edited by Anne Schulz
ISBN 1-882688-01-5

Falling Wallendas
by Michael R. Brown
ISBN 1-882688-02-3

Schoolyard of Broken Dreams
by Marvin Tate
ISBN 1-882688-03-1

Fallout
by Kyoko Mori
ISBN 1-882688-04-X

Night Song
by Andres Rodríguez
ISBN 1-882688-05-8

A Snake in the Heart:
Poems and Music by Chicago Spoken
Word Performers
ISBN 1-882688-06-6 (CD)

Love's Instruments
by Melvin Dixon
ISBN 1-882688-07-4

El Grupo McDonald's
by Nick Carbó
ISBN 1-882688-08-2

Armadillo Charm
by Carlos Cumpían
ISBN 1-882688-09-0

Same Blue Chevy
by Gale Renee Walden
ISBN 1-882688-10-4

Looking for a Soft Place to Land
by Cin Salach
ISBN 1-882688-11-2

Body of Life
by Elizabeth Alexander
ISBN 1-882688-12-0

The Loves of Ricardo
by Ricardo Sánchez
ISBN 1-882688-13-9 (hardcover); ISBN
1-882688-14-7 (paperback)

Exquisite Politics
by Denise Duhamel
& Maureen Seaton
ISBN 1-882688-15-5

Leaving Gary
by John Sheehan
ISBN 1-882688-16-3

Talismán
by Afaa M. Weaver
ISBN 1-882688-17-1

shards of light/astillas de luz
edited by Olivia Maciel
ISBN 1-882688-18-X

You Come Singing
by Virgil Suárez
ISBN 1-882688-19-8

Blues Narratives
by Sterling D. Plumpp
ISBN 1-882688-20-1

Muscular Music
by Terrance Hayes
ISBN 1-882688-21-X

Power Lines: A Decade of Poetry
from Chicago's Guild Complex,
edited by Julie Parson- Nesbitt,
Luis J. Rodríguez, and Michael Warr
ISBN 1-882688-22-8

The Relief of America
by Diane Glancy
ISBN 1-882688-23-6

Secret Asian Man
by Nick Carbó
ISBN 1-882688-24-4

Bum Town
by Tony Fitzpatrick
ISBN 1-882688-25-2

Rise
by A. Van Jordan
ISBN 1-882688-26-0

The Mean Days
by Anne-Marie Cusac
ISBN 1-882688-27-9

Singing the Bones Together
by Angela Shannon
ISBN 1-882688-28-7

My Sweet Unconditional
by ariel robello
ISBN 1-882688-29-5

Dream of a Word: The Tia Chucha
Press Poetry Anthology
edited by Quraysh Ali Lansana
and Toni Asante Lightfoot
ISBN 1-882688-30-9

CHAPBOOKS

mississippi [r]evolutions
by Zada Johnson
(a Luis J. Rodriguez Chapbook)

30 seconds
by Mike Puican
(a Luis J. Rodriguez Chapbook)

American Vignette
by Josie Raney
(a Richard H. Driehaus Chapbook)

ABOUT THE CONTRIBUTORS

ELIZABETH ALEXANDER is the author of four poetry collections, including *American Sublime,* as well as a collection of essays, *The Black Interior.* She lives in New Haven, Connecticut.

MICHAEL R. BROWN has published his poetry, fiction, travel articles, and columns in wide-ranging periodicals all over the world. He holds a Ph.D. in English and Education from the University of Michigan.

LISA BUSCANI has been featured in poetry anthologies such as *Alive from the NuYorican Poets Café* (Holt) and *Word Up* (Keyporter Books/EMI). She has appeared on HBO, CNN, PBS, Much Music and NPR.

NICK CARBÓ received an MFA in Creative Writing from Sara Lawrence College and has served as Resident Poet at Bucknell University and Writer in Residence at The American University.

CARLOS CUMPÍAN is a veteran Chicano writer. Cumpián examines American realities absent from mainstream poetry. Although he hails from San Antonio, Texaztlan, Cumpián has planted firm roots in the Midwest. Cumpián was named among the Chicago Public Library's "Top Ten" most requested poets and his poetry has been published by some of the country's spirited small press magazines as well as in numerous anthologies.

ANNE-MARIE CUSAC is the author of *The Mean Days* (Tia Chucha Press, 2001). She is the Investigative Reporter for The Progressive Magazine and is currently working on a book about American punishment for Yale University Press.

MELVIN DIXON grew up in Stamford, CT. He received his B.A. from Wesleyan University in 1971 and a doctorate at Brown University. Melvin's books include *Change of Territory,* poems; the novels *Trouble the Waters* and *Vanishing Rooms;* and *Ride out the Wilderness: Geography and Identity in Afro-American Literature,* literary criticism. He passed away on October 26, 1992 of an AIDS-related illness.

DENISE DUHAMEL is the author of four books of poems. She is the recipient of a New York Foundation for the Arts Fellowship. Denise recently won first place in the Crab Orchard Award Series in poetry, sponsored by the Crab Orchard Review.

TONY FITZPATRICK was born in Chicago in 1958 and lives with his wife and children. He is also an artist with a gist for imagery and detailed drawing in both large and small print.

DIANE GLANCY is a professor at Macalester College. Her latest books are *In-Between Places*, a collection of essays; *The Dance Partner, stories of the Ghost Dance;* and *Rooms: New & Selected Poems.*

MARY KATHLEEN HAWLEY was born in Milwaukee and has worked as a teacher, translator, journalist and editor. Hawley has also helped to organize the Chicago Poetry Festival.

TERRANCE HAYES is a native of South Carolina. He received his MFA from the University of Pittsburgh and has published a range of literary journals and anthologies.

DAVID HERNÁNDEZ has published several books of poetry and has written and edited numerous anthologies. He has received grants and recognition from the Illinois Arts Council, Chicago's Office of Fine Arts among others.

JEAN HOWARD participated in the original development of the internationally acclaimed "Poetry Slam" Her poetry has appeared in *Harper's Magazine, The Burning World, Spoon River Review,* and the *Chicago Tribune,* among seventy other literary publications. Her book, *Dancing in Your Mother's Skin,* is a collaborative work with photographer Alice Hargrave.

ZADA JOHNSON is a doctoral student in the Department of Anthropology at the University of Chicago studying Afro-Caribbean ritual performance in Cuba and New Orleans. Her poetry has appeared in *Creativity Magazine, Esi Anthology of Women Writers* and *Warpland Anthology of Black Literature and Ideas.*

A. VAN JORDAN is a founding member of the Poison Clan Collective and a member of the Cave Canem Workshop. He has taught at Warren Wilson in Asheville, NC; Prince George's Community College in Largo, MD; and with AmeriCorps WritersCorps in Washington, DC. Van Jordan is the author of *M-A-C-N-O-L-I-A-* and has received the PEN Oakland/Josephine Miles Award for his previous book *Rise.* He currently teaches at the University of Texas, Austin campus.

KYOKO MORI is the author of three novels (*Shizuko's Daughter, One Bird; Stone Field, True Arrow*) and two nonfiction books (*The Dream of Water; Polite Lies*) as well as her book of poetry, *Fallout,* from Tia Chucha Press. She teaches creative writing at George Mason University.

DWIGHT OKITA. After working in poetry and theater for many years, these days Dwight Okita has turned his attention to fiction. He just finished writing his first novel, *The Prospect of My Arrival,* and is seeking an agent.

STERLING D. PLUMPP is a poet and educator from Clinton, Mississippi. He has written numerous books, including *Hornman, Harriet Tubman, Ornate with Smoke, Blues: The Story Always Untold,* and *Half Black, Half Blacker.* Plumpp is currently Professor Emeritus at Chicago State University where he teaches in the MFA program.

ROHAN B PRESTON received a degree from Yale University in English Literature. He has taught journalism and parliamentary debate in programs at Wellesley College.

MIKE PUICAN has published widely including the journals *Luna, Crab Orchard Review, Another Chicago Magazine, The Bloomsbury Review* and *Spoon River Review.*

JOSIE RANEY holds an undergraduate degree from Carleton College (1994) and an MFA in poetry from University of Virginia (1999). As a Fulbright Scholar in Budapest, Hungary, she translated a selection of contemporary Hungarian poems. Her work has appeared in a number of publications including *Five Points* and *Water-Stone.*

ARIEL ROBELLO is a former Pen West Emerging Voices Fellow and founder of Full Moon Phases. She works as an adult ESL educator, a freelance writer and poetry teacher in high schools.

ANDRES RODRÍGUEZ is a second-generation Mexican American. He is a native of Kansas City, born to the legacy of the migration of farm workers to that region. He studied English literature at the University of Iowa, Stanford University, and the University of California, Santa Cruz.

LUIS J. RODRÍGUEZ has emerged as one of the leading Chicano writers in the country with ten nationally published books in memoir, fiction, non-fiction, children's literature, and poetry. He is founder-editor of Tia Chucha Press and a co-founder of Tia Chucha's Café & Centro Cultural.

CIN SALACH has been performing her words around the country since 1987. Cin is also the cofounder of the Loofah Method and Betty's Mouth— two poetic, duetic, multi-mediatic performance groups.

RICARDO SÁNCHEZ is considered one of the fathers of the Chicano literary genre and is one of the most published and anthologized Chicano writers.

MAUREEN SEATON'S most recent collection is *Venus Examines Her Breast* (Carnegie Mellon University Press, 2004), winner of the Publishing Triangle's Audre Lorde Award.

ANGELA SHANNON has won a poetry fellowship from Illinois Arts Council and a Mentor Award from the Loft in Minneapolis, where she has also taught. She received an MFA in poetry from Warren Wilson College.

JOHN SHEEHAN's poetry is rooted in the social activism of Vatican II, and the civil rights and anti-war movements of the sixties. Sheehan's poetry collection, *Leaving Gary,* published by Tia Chucha Press, confronts issues of race, class, religion, and the media – with keen observations of place, people, and time.

PATRICIA SMITH is the author of the poetry volumes *Close to Death; Big Towns, Big Talk;* and *Life According to Motown.* She has also authored *Africans in America,* the companion book to the PBS series; the award-winning children's book *Janna and the Kings;* and the upcoming poetry book *Teahouse of the Almighty.* She is currently at work on *Fixed on a Furious Star,* a biography of Harriet Tubman, and the young adult novel, *The Journey of Willie J.*

VIRGIL SUÁREZ is the author of five books of fiction; a memoir titled *Spared Angola: Memories from a Cuban-American Childhood;* and two books of poetry: *You Come Singing* and *Garabato Poems.* He teaches creative writing at Florida State University in Tallahassee, Florida.

MARVIN TATE is an author and performance poet. His first book of poems, *School Yard of Broken Dreams,* was published in 1994. Presently he is diligently finishing up his second book of poems and recording a solo CD.

GAIL RENEE WALDEN was born in Urbana, Illinois and grew up on the South Side of Chicago. She took a B.A. in music therapy and an MFA in writing from the University of Arizona.

MICHAEL WARR is a recipient of a Gwendolyn Brooks Significant Illinois Poets Award. He has been published and translated by the San Francisco-based poetry magazine, *Compages,* as well as *Hammers, Libido,* and *Literati Internacionale.*

AFAA MICHAEL WEAVER is a poet, playwright, short fiction writer, and journalist. His latest of nine collections of poetry include *Multitudes, The Ten Lights of God,* and *Sandy Point.*

ABOUT THE EDITORS

QURAYSH ALI LANSANA is author of three poetry books, including *They Shall Run: Harriet Tubman Poems* (Third World Press, 2004) a children's book; and editor of five anthologies, including *Role Call: A Generational Anthology of Social and Political Black Literature and Art* (Third World Press, 2001). He is Director of the Gwendolyn Brooks Center for Black Literature and Creative Writing at Chicago State University, where he is also an Assistant Professor of English and Creative Writing. Quraysh serves as Associate Editor-Poetry for Black Issues Book Review and earned a MFA in Creative Writing at New York University.

TONI ASANTE LIGHTFOOT, educated at Howard University, George Washington University and Cave Canem Poetry Workshop, is a seasoned creative writing instructor – having taught through ETA Creative Arts Foundation, Young Chicago Authors, WritersCorp, and the Guild Complex, where she was also Outreach Manager. Toni has also developed curriculum that highlights the interdisciplinary uses of poetry in the classroom. She contributes regularly to *Black Issues Book Review,* has been featured on Def Poetry Jam, and performed her poetry at The National Theater, The Lincoln Theater, and The Democratic National Committee Headquarters. She is a 2005 Soul Mountain Retreat Fellow and winner of the 2005 Gwendolyn Brooks Open Mic Award.